VISION OF CANADA 2020

Save Canadian Medicare and Money

E L I Z A B E T H   E L S I E   H A N N A F O R D

iUniverse, Inc.
Bloomington

Vision of Canada 2020
Save Canadian Medicare and Money

iUniverse books may be ordered through booksellers or by contacting:

iUniverse
1663 Liberty Drive
Bloomington, IN 47403
www.iuniverse.com
1-800-Authors (1-800-288-4677)

ISBN: 978-1-4502-8052-5 (pbk)
ISBN: 978-1-4502-8053-2 (cloth)
ISBN: 978-1-4502-8054-9 (ebk)

Printed in the United States of America

iUniverse rev. date: 1/3/2011

Acknowlegment

There are not enough words to describe this man. He is kind, considerate, hospitable, courteous, amiable, beneficent, good hearted, good natured, gracious, tender, lenient, merciful, obliging, charitable, philanthropic, accommodating and humanitarian.

For the past few years, as I got weaker in body due to my advancing age, Dr. Farouk Chebib has looked after my every need, physically, mentally and financially. He thinks of everything big and small, things that I need to do in order to have all my business in order. He sends me regularly a neatly typed report summarizing the status of my affairs and a list reminding me of the things that have to be done, bills to be paid, phone calls I have to make, etc. Recently he had double by-pass surgery. Even at that time, his main concern was to see that I had a suitable picture for the book cover and little concern for his own recovery. That's been Farouk ever since I met him. He's always looking after my every need.

Dr. Chebib knew that my last wish and desire would be to see my book published. When he offered to help me get it published, I felt that it was a God send. As he worked with me day after day, I came to realize the implications and the requirements of getting a manuscript ready for publishing. My story line was terribly disjointed and required numerous re-editing to make logical sense. He went through several drafts and corrections to the manuscript without adding any of his material to it so that I get full credit for every word in the book. He simply acted as an editor and communicated with the publishers. Farouk was always thoughtful in making sure that I understood all that he was trying to achieve for a successful book.

There is no end to my appreciation of this man's talent. The knowledge and wisdom that I gained in my advanced years is a vast contrast to his Ph. D.

How I ever deserved to have such a good friend like Farouk is something I fail to understand. I do know that although there may be others who have as good a friend; they will never have one that is better.

With my best wishes for your good health and happiness.

Lovingly, Elsie
October 25, 2010

Elizabeth Elsie Hannaford

To:

Sri Sri Ravi-Shankar

and

W. Brett Wilson

Contents

Dedications

This book is dedicated to very influential people whose influence will be felt worldwide. They are W. Brett Wilson, Sri Sri Ravi-Shankar, Francois Gauthier, Oprah Winfrey, Bill Gates, Warren Buffett, Sir Richard Branson, Dr Mark Winston, Celine Dion, Honorable John Ralston Saul and Dean Graham Scoles, University of Saskatchewan, and others.

As well to the following great people:

Adriana Clarkson
Andrew Bacevich (Boston University)
Bill Gates
Chip Coffey
Cindy Klassen
Daniel Tammet
David Northcott
Dean Graham Scoles
Doris Kearns Goodwin
Dr. Andrew Weaver
Dr. David Suzuki
Dr. Dongfeng Sun
Dr. Farouk Chebib
Dr. Mark Winston
Dr. Michael Moore

Dr. Yali Bai
Ed Finn
Farley Mowat
Francis Russell
Gail Asper Patterson
Glenn Murray
Helen & Pat Robertson
Her Excellency Michaëlle Jean
Jimmy Carter
John Ralston Saul
Justice Emmet Hall
Justin Trudeau
Kim Campbell
Let. Gov. Hon. Phillip Lee
Margaret Atwood
Margaret Trudeau
Marshall Kluke
Maurice Strong
Michael J Fox
Michael J. Hall
Oprah Winfrey
People of this Earth
Prime Minister Stephen Harper
Ronald N. Goodwin
Severn Suzuki
Sir Richard Branson
Stan P. Millan
Superstar Celine Dion
Susan Ann Thompson
Walter Gretsky
Warren Buffett
Wayne Gretsky
William Neville

And to

Famous 5: National Council of Women of Canada
President of the Canadian Medical Association
Prime Minister of China
Prime Minister of India

And to the following deceased individuals:

Art Buchwald
Cam & Myrtle Robertson
Cora Hind
Duff Roblin
Gabrielle Roy
Izzy Asper
June Callwood
Leo Mol
Marshal McLuhan
Nellie McClung
Pearl Weller
Pierre Elliot Trudeau
Roy Romanow
Stephen Juba
Terry Fox
Tommy Douglas
William Norrie

In appreciation to their greatness, accomplishments, passions and kindness, I take great pleasure in dedicating my book, "Vision of Canada 2010 – Saving Medicare and money" to all the people mentioned above and in the following chapters. Humanity and I owe you a great deal.

Elsie Hannaford

Forward

This book is based on "The Art of Living" Foundation, whose founder, Sri Sri Ravi-Shankar, is a world renowned spiritual leader as well as a founding member along with several other world leaders of the International Association for Human Values. He has been a featured speaker at many forums across the world including the European Parliament, the U.N. Millennium Summit and the World Economic Forum in Davos, Switzerland.

The Art of Living Foundation, founded in 1982 by His Holiness Sri Sri Ravi Shankar, is one of the world's largest humanitarian organizations, initiating numerous social projects in more than 146 countries. The Foundation is an international humanitarian and educational Non-Governmental Organization (NGO) in special consultative status with the Economic Social Council (ECOSOC) of the United Nations (UN).

Sri Sri Ravi Shankar is an internationally respected peacemaker and has inspired many educational and charitable organizations and projects around the globe. Every year He addresses people in more than 40 countries and His programs have touched the lives of over 50 million people worldwide.

W. Brett Wilson is our proudest and most patriotic Canadian who has been honored by over a dozen prominent organizations. Kindly refer Charter I, "People to Admire" for some of the achievements of these two great individuals.

The philosophy of the author may be summarized as follows:

1. W. Brett Wilson is the most powerful citizen in the world.

2. Canada has the most combined resources of unoccupied territory, green space, water, grains wheat, canola, flax, barley, oats, mustard and minerals than any other country in the world.

3. Canada will ban manufacturing of fast foods. Those companies manufacturing of fast foods will manufacture healthy food instead.

4. Canada will implement a strict building code of 4 stories saving of green space. Extended family living will be encouraged. The first floor will be for the family, the second floor for their grandparents, the third floor for guests or for storage. The fourth floor will be for storage of dried fruits, seeds and vegetables. Back yard can be used for outdoor garden growing as well as for the enjoyment of being outdoors.

5. People who cannot grow their own food will buy from suppliers who may import food grown in unpolluted soil, from China, India, Thailand etc.

6. Those countries wishing to join Canada shall banish manufacture of fast food, the cause of obesity and implement the purchase of safe and healthy food.

7. Homes of people will be checked to ensure they don't contain banished or unauthorized food.

8. Employ dietician to watch for proper eating habits recommending small portions and regular bowel movements using Metamucil and lots of water.

In writing this book the author consulted with the works of many people and organizations, among which are:

- Francois Gauthier
- Dr. Farouk S. Chebib
- University of Saskatchewan
- Winnipeg Free Press
- Associated Press
- Elder Larry Monkman
- MacLean's Magazine
- University of Victoria knowledge by Shannon McCullum
- Los Angeles Times
- Wikipedia.org
- Google Search Engine
- Linklin.com

Introduction

"United we stand (succeed),
Divided we fall (fail)."

"Vision of Canada 2020, Saving Canadian Medicare and Money" is a planned method of bringing about world peace and spirituality. It is a method based on these ten concepts:

1. A Canadian alliance with China and India (an exchange of millions of immigrants for huge Canadian resources of food, oil, water, technology etc)

    A concept of reciprocal trust and cooperation – not competition.

    Canada welcomes all other countries and people. No one will be turned away. Immigrants with problems will be treated until healed. Those who immigrate and who need help with problems like drug abuse will receive help until that problem is resolved.

2. The Art of Living Foundation founded by His Holiness Sri Sri Ravi Shankar, a world renowned Guru (see internet for credentials)

    "In the Art of Living Program, the International Association for Human Values, through its 5H Program, assists in eradicating misery and in transforming society. For Guruji, 'Human life is a great and rare gift, and all people on this planet should have the chance to express through their lives the full potential of their humanness.' This means claiming their birthright to a disease-free body and a stress-free mind, which in turn means living lives that express human values such as compassion, generosity, and ethic of service and caring for all life. Thus, He feels that social transformation begins with a happy and healthy individual who has attained a decent standard of living and has received essential education in health, hygiene, and life skills." (Please refer to <u>The Guru of Joy: Sri Sri Ravi-Shankar and the Art of Living</u>, p. 155, by Francois Gautier.)

All aspects of endeavor in this book are designed to demonstrate, promote and practice the art of living as founded by His Holiness, Sri Sri Ravi-Shankar

3. Obesity in Children and the harmful effect of DDT found in breast milk

4. Bees: Social Insects by Dr. Mark Winston (see internet for credentials)

    This theory reminds me of the North American Aboriginal philosophical concept of hierarchy and interdependence. Also it seems to me this concept is compatible with the Art of Living concept.

5. A Fair Country – Telling Truths about Canada, by Honorable John Ralston Saul.

    According to John Ralston Saul we have inherited Métis culture and as a result we are all Métis people.

6. Embracing the Wide Sky – by Daniel Tammet

7. We Can Have Peace in the Holy Land – by Jimmy Carter

8. Living with Parkinson's – by Michael J Fox

9. Crows - Most intelligent animals. They sense other people's language – Based on research done by the University of Oxford England.

Crows have an unspoken motto: Sticks and stones may break my bones, but they sure can come in handy. Two new studies unveil the ability of at least some crows to use tools in sophisticated ways, without training, to obtain food.

Crows' problem-solving feats in these studies underscore a substantial intelligence that has attracted relatively little scientific attention, according to both research teams.

Scientists have previously noted tool use among members of the crow family, or corvids, including dropping stones on intruders or prey and using paper as a rake and sponge. But few birds outside this family display comparable behavior, and researchers have largely concentrated on the extensive, flexible tool practices of chimpanzees and other nonhuman primates. Evidence from apes and monkeys, as well as other large-brained, social animals such as dolphins, has debunked the traditional view that tool use is a defining human characteristic.

In one study, appearing in the Aug. 25 Current Biology, zoologists Christopher Bird of the University of Cambridge in England and Nathan Emery of Queen Mary, University of London report that captive rooks--members of the crow family--rapidly learn on their own to use stones to obtain food. The rooks dropped stones into a tube containing water in order to raise the water level and bring a floating worm within reach. This behavior recalls one of Aesop's fables, in which a thirsty crow plunked rocks into a pitcher to raise the water level high enough for a drink.

10. Octopus – Research shows that they have a high level

of intelligence compared to other animals. Ex: They are capable of opening a jar in order to get the contents out.

An octopus in a German zoo has learned to open jars of shrimps by copying staff - and is now showing off her skills to visitors. Five-month-old Frida opens the jars by pressing her body on the lid and grasping the sides with her eight tentacles. She unscrews the lid by repeatedly twisting her body. "Depending on how tight the lid is, it takes her anything from 10 seconds to an hour to get it off," said Frank Mueller, head of the aquarium at the Hellabrunn Zoo in Munich. She opens the jars before the public at feeding time twice a week. Mr. Mueller said he taught Frida the trick after he remembered seeing octopuses accomplishing feats of dexterity while he was diving in Morocco - where Frida originated.

CHAPTER I:
PEOPLE TO ADMIRE

The People of the Earth

Have faith and you will find within yourself a good and happier person.

Sri Sri Ravi-Shankar

He is Founder of the International Art of Living Foundation with centers in over 140 countries in the world with an ever growing following of millions of people across the globe. A tireless traveler, He has addressed the United Nations, The World Economic Forum and bright young minds at Harvard University. In a world torn by strife, He has carried the eternal message of love and revival of human values. People from all walks of life seek His blessing and advice. He exudes love, innocence and joy in every gesture. At the same time He has practical answers for all the problems plaguing us today - Terrorism, war, political dysfunction and personal conflicts. The programs He has devised have miraculous healing powers that lead to a world of true spirituality - Guru of Joy.

W. Brett Wilson

Our proudest and most patriotic Canadian who has been honored by the following organizations;

Canada's Top 4o under 40 (Caldwell - 1997)

Top 20 deal Makers in Canada (Globe & Mail -1999)

Top 10 list of M&A specialists in Canada (Globe & Mail – 2000)

Management Alumni Excellence (MAX) Award, University of Calgary, Haskaune School of Business (2003)

International Legacy of Honor, Young Presidents Organization – recognizing the global YPO leader who best exemplifies commitment to excellence in business, community orientation and ideals of YPO (2004)

Spirit of Giving Award (Association of Fundraising Professionals – 2005

University of Calgary Top 40 Alumni (2006- 2007)

Calgary's Person of the year (Avenue Magazine – 2007)

University of Saskatchewan Top 100 Alumni (2007)

Distinguished Lecturer, CJ Mackenzie Banquet, University of Saskatchewan College of Engineering (2008)

Canadian Youth Business Foundation Nation Builder Award – 2009

For further information please see biography, University of Saskatchewan, Mr. Wilson's alma mater.

He has sponsored many Canadians and given them rise to fame and success. I do not wish to discredit those people chosen as important Canadians but they in no way contributed anywhere near what Mr. Wilson did and continues to do. In my view Mr. Brett Wilson is the "Golden Boy" of the Olympics and the most Patriotic citizen.

I have contributed to the University of Saskatchewan for a number of years because I believe the work they do paves the way to establishing the goals of my book (manuscript) which are to establish close relationships with India and China by forming an alliance and making Canada the most powerful nation and the envy of the rest of the world.

I do not want one cent for myself. My only goal is to be able to help others by having the sponsorship of medical faculties in Canada. This sponsorship will enable students who otherwise would not be able to enter the Faculty of Medicine. It would also ensure the sponsor of his or her healthcare for the rest of his or her life. Canadian healthcare is of worldwide reputation, leading in medical research at the Winnipeg Research Centre in Winnipeg, Manitoba Canada.

Dr. Farouk Chebib, PhD

Dr. Chebib is a proud Canadian, an outstanding scientist and a retired University professor who has dedicated his retirement years to helping those whose lives he could make better.

Dr. Chebib worked as a research scientist at his University for 25 years. He attained the rank of a Full Professor before he took his early retirement. In his "retirement years", he taught University overseas for three years before he secured his dream job as Principal Scientist in the Space Division of a large corporation in the United State manufacturing the space shuttle boosters for NASA. He re-retired after 10 years. In his "second retirement period", he worked for six more years as a consultant in the aerospace industry for many of the larger manufacturing companies in the United States.

When he finally retired he returned to his home in Winnipeg.

Dr. Mark Winston

Winston's major areas of research interest include life history, caste structure, and reproduction in social insects, pheromones of honeybees and their pests, crop pollination and pollination biology, and bee management. Current projects include:

1. Pheromone effects on worker ovary development.
2. The evolution of multiple mating in honey bees.
3. Bumble bee drifting and orientation studies.
4. Pollinator life history and management in managed greenhouse tomato systems.
5. Impact of genetically modified pollens and novel pesticides on non-target wild bees.
6. Interactions between agricultural practices, nearby plant communities, and pollinator diversity and encouraging conservation programs.

He also is continuing basic studies of honey bee behaviors associated with swarming, temporal polytheism, and foraging, as well as other bee keeping and pollination management projects.

Dr. Andrew Weaver

Climate changes, that's a fact. Twenty thousand years ago, Victoria was covered by kilometer-thick ice and the average global temperature was four degrees colder.

Now, with overwhelming evidence that human activities are increasing global temperatures, University of Victoria climatologist

Andrew Weaver is asking a key question: can the study of past climate changes help us predict future ones?

Understanding Earth's climate system is no trivial task. Climate is incredibly complex, involving interactions between the atmosphere, ocean, biosphere, and cryosphere (snow and ice surfaces).

One approach researchers can take is to design sophisticated computer models to simulate past, present and future climates. These models act as virtual laboratories, allowing researchers to perform climate experiments that can't be done in the real world.

At University of Victoria, Weaver has built one of the most sophisticated climate modeling facilities on the planet, featuring one of the world's fastest supercomputers. Several years ago, he and his climate modeling group developed an Earth system climate model, now used by researchers around the world to study long term climate change.

One climate puzzle that Weaver is investigating with the model is how past climate changes are linked to the global carbon cycle. Carbon dioxide and methane are continuously exchanged between the atmosphere, oceans and biosphere. Understanding this exchange is essential to predicting how increasing carbon emissions will affect future climates.

"We know that carbon dioxide and methane have amplified climate change during glacial cycles," says Weaver. "We're using our model to study how the ocean and land plants absorb atmospheric carbon and to investigate how changes in the carbon cycle have interacted with climatic changes over the last 650,000 years."

One of the key missing links in the carbon cycle is permafrost, which is basically a huge frozen carbon reserve. "It's an important part of the carbon cycle and global climate system," notes Weaver, "yet it has received little detailed attention in the climate modeling world."

To this end, Weaver's team plans to be one of the first research groups in the world to add a permafrost component to a model that is full linked to the carbon cycle.

Permafrost is of special interest to Canada because it underlies more than half the country's land mass. In a warming climate, melting permafrost will release large amounts of carbon into the atmosphere, further accelerating global warming. It will also result in the loss of wildlife habitat, and disrupt transportation and northern infrastructure.

Weaver says the next generation of his climate model will address the influence of climate on human evolution-much like it's now being used to examine the influence of humans on climate evolution.

This and subsequent models will continue to help industry and governments develop realistic policy options for dealing with the inevitable effect of climate change.

"The evidence keeps mounting that most climate warming observed over the last 50 years is due to human activities," he says, "this is acknowledged by the world's leading scientists and sends a strong signal to governments that informed policy is urgently needed to determine a course of action for the future." (Excerpt from University of Victoria Knowledge by Shannon McCallum) PostScript: Carbon dioxide is the major greenhouse gas released into the atmosphere by human activities. Since the start of the industrial revolution, carbon dioxide concentrations in the atmosphere have increased by 36% and are still rising. UVic's Andrew Weaver is a world leader in climate dynamics and the Canada Research Chair in Climate Modeling and analysis. He was also a lead author of the UN Intergovernmental Panel on Climate Change's climate assessment held in February 2007, which directed international policies related to global warming. UVic's climate modeling group consists of three faculty members, five research associates and 14 graduate students. Members come from all over the world, from backgrounds as diverse as physics, mathematics, engineering, oceanography and geology. They work closely with scientists in the Canadian Centre for Climate Modeling and Analysis, a division of Environment Canada, housed at UVic. UVic researchers were awarded more than $84 million in external research grants and contracts in 2005-06, up nearly 150% since 2001-02.

Ed Finn

Editor and author of "The Right is Wrong and the Left is Right" and Canadian Centre for Policy Alternatives Monitor. Spent his life struggling for social justice, never giving in to his right wing opponents but countering them and devising fair and viable alternatives. His ideas continue to inform and inspire others in the ongoing struggle for a better world. He is one of the first writers and editors to challenge corporate power and expose its ruinous effects. His appeal for aid and my sympathy for his wish led to writing this book. Little did I know how much it would entail. I thought it was a simple favor to someone who worked really hard and needed help.

Oprah Winfrey

Oprah, identified by her first name only: a custom usually reserved for Royal families, is a famous and very talented celebrity. She is very open and honest. She is extremely generous in sharing her life experience both good and bad: sometimes painful but always honest. People can relate and empathize with her easily and comfortably. This is the reason she is so extremely popular and well known by the vast majority of people of North American and all over the world. In view of her humble origins this is a phenomenally enviable accomplishment. Her sensitivity to a given situation creates empathy by the observer bringing her closer to our heart. Her continual efforts to find ways of helping people to learn about things they may never have discovered on their own and her ability to help people to solve their problems by showing them what they can do to resolve them is remarkable.

Here are some examples:

1. How to stay within your budget

2. How to organize your clothes closet or to organize your bedroom

3. Which cleaning products are best suited for cleaning clothes, appliances, floors, etc

4. There is no end to these how to's.

This strategy in Oprah's program is helpful and practical and is a big success and increases her popularity. Her potential is endless, her TV viewers look forward to seeing what's next on her programs. She has thrilled her audiences with ultra exclusive gifts that they could not afford and she has had these delivered to their homes free of charge or worry. Oprah's philanthropy extends beyond the financial. She gives so much of herself. She is also instrumental in promoting others to be philanthropic. Her contribution and accomplishment is worldwide and the envy of all people. Canadians are honored, proud and humble in dedicating this book to Oprah.

Bill Gates

The world's most generous philanthropist has promised to dispense ninety five percent of his wealth (over fifty billion dollars) to worthwhile charities before he dies. He set up with his wife Linda the Bill and Linda Gates Foundation, the largest of its kind to distribute needed funds to worthy groups and causes especially in poor countries. Gates has a social conscience and has put his wealth to constructive use. He uses his money to do what governments can't or won't do. He has shown the world what to do with its money to make a difference and a better world. His legacy will live on long after he has gone. He has left his mark on earth forever, never to be forgotten.

Warren Buffett

Warren Buffet displayed an amazing aptitude for both money and business at a very early age. He has an uncanny ability to calculate columns of numbers off the top of his head – a feat with which Warren still amazes business colleagues today. His mentor, Bill Graham at Columbia University introduced him to simple yet profound investment principles. He has mastered the art of investing. Known as the "Oracle of Omaha", Buffett is chairman of Berkshire Hathaway and arguably the greatest investor of all time. His net worth is estimated at $62 Billion making him the richest man in the world. Buffett is equally well known for his philanthropic work. His vision and compassion have opened the world's eyes to social justice. Recently Warren Buffett announced his decision to donate some $37 billion worth of shares in his firm Berkshire Hathaway to 5 charitable foundations. The largest recipient (receiving some $31 billion) will be the Bill and Melinda Gates Foundation, which specializes, in global health and education projects.

That one solitary human being has nearly forty billion dollars to dispose of, with a good deal left over, is appalling in itself, at a time when 1.1 billion people, one-fifth of the world's population, live on less than $1 a day and some 3 billion on less than $2. The planet's three wealthiest individuals in 2005 (including Messrs. Buffett and Gates) had greater wealth than the combined gross domestic product of the world's 48 poorest nations.

There is, in any event, something intrinsically degrading and demeaning about philanthropy. A society in need of philanthropists is one rooted in inequality, in which the deprivation of the many is supposedly addressed by the largesse of the few. No one can seriously suggest that social problems will be solved in this manner. Especially in America, where an aristocracy has taken shape before our eyes over the past decade and the Bush administration is taking blind, reckless measures to eliminate all restrictions on the accumulation of personal wealth.

As for Mr. Buffett himself, there are no doubt immense personal contradictions in his life. If one takes the media accounts at face value, he seems an honest and civilized man. Among many unsavory, rotten types, he appears to stand out as something of an exception. He has liberal views on social issues and has put his money to use in a number of worthy causes. He lives modestly in a home bought decades ago.

Canadians owe Warren Buffett gratitude and thanks. The ultimate goal of this book is to strive for a happier life filled with contentment, respect for all humanity and all other creatures we live with on this earth. Mr. Buffett has shown by his deeds the way to fulfill that dream and Canadians are honored to dedicate this book to him.

Sir Richard Branson

You are a neat guy! The most enterprising adventurists in the world. One of the most influential people in the world. Recipient of the United Nations Correspondents Association "Citizen of the World" for supporting environmental and humanitarian causes. There is nothing you can't do! You are self-made; self-educated, "with an honorary degree!" self-entrepreneur – "Knighted"!

You have proved that in order to help others you must make money first. Not everyone who has lots of money feels an obligation to help those in need. That's where you differ! Your philanthropic generosity is overwhelming! "Virgin Unite"- getting others to help where it is so desperately needed! You think of everything!

Your choice of Virgin for a name for your projects and your vision of establishing life on a new planet is exciting. Canadians have a vision. You have inspired them with the courage to carry on in spite of the many difficulties to make this a better world. Canadians are truly honored to dedicate this book to one who deserves so much more.

Andrew Bacevich

Andrew J. Bacevich is a Professor of International Relations at Boston University, Former Director of its Center for International Relations and author of several books, including *American Empire: the Realities and Consequences of US Diplomacy* (2002) and *The New American Militarism: How American s are Seduced by War* (2005). He has been a "persistent, vocal critic of the US occupation of Iraq, calling the conflict a catastrophic failure." In March 2007, he described George W Bush's endorsement of such "preventive wars" as "immoral, illicit and imprudent." He was robbed of a son because he died fighting in the Iraq war in May of 2007.

Leo Mol

Born Leonid Molodozhanyn in Polonne, Ukraine, Mol studied sculpture at the Leningrad Academy of Arts from 1936 to 1940. Following the German invasion of the Soviet Union he moved to Germany where he was influenced by Arno Breker. In 1945, he moved to The Hague, and in December, 1948, he and his wife, Magareth (whom he married in 1943), emigrated to Winnipeg, Manitoba.

More than three hundred of Mol's works are displayed in the Leo Mol Sculpture Garden in Winnipeg's Assiniboine Park. The garden was unveiled in 1992 and has been expanded twice since. It is supported by private donations, and Mol personally donated most of the sculpture. In 2002, his sculpture Lumberjacks was featured on a Canadian postage stamp.

He was always known as a particularly prolific artist and some of his most famous works include likenesses of three different Popes which stand in museums in the Vatican. He also has a sculpture of Taras Shevchenko on display on Washington's Embassy Row.

Other important subjects who Mol sculpted include members of the Group of 7, A. J. Casson, A.Y. Jackson and Frederick Varley. Mol also sculpted Sir Winston Churchill 1966, Peter Kuch, Dwight D. Eisenhower 1965, John F. Kennedy 1969, Elizabeth Bradford Holbrook ca. 1970, Terry Fox 1982. On Parliament Hill in Ottawa stands his impressive over life-size standing portrait figure of Prime Minister John George Diefenbaker 1985. Also on Parliament Hill stands an impressive bronze statue of Queen Elizabeth II.

Mol died July 4, 2009, at the Tache Centre medical facility in Winnipeg, Manitoba. He was 94.

Honors:

In 1989, he was made an Officer of the Order of Canada. In 2000, he was awarded the Order of Manitoba. He was a member of the Royal Canadian Academy of Arts.

He received honorary degrees from the University of Winnipeg, the University of Alberta and the University of Manitoba.

Mol's was also made an Honorary Academician of the Canadian Portrait Academy (Hon. CPA) in 2000.

Dr. Yali Bai

Dr. Yali Bai Graduated from Heze Medical School in China in 1981. Her major was traditional Chinese Medicine and Acupuncture. Before she moved to Canada, she practiced acupuncture at Heze Chinese Medicine Hospital for 16 years. She immigrated to Canada in 1997 and opened an Acupuncture Clinic at Winnipeg in 2000.

Dr. Bai is an exceptional therapist in acupuncture, Chinese Massage, Herbal Medicine and Electromagnetic Therapy. She is a wise counselor, faithful, protective, and generous friend. Dr. Yali Bai has been treating me for several years now and has restored feeling in my legs making them feel more normal. In her wisdom she constantly found ways to placate me when I am upset about some incident. She maintains her cool professionalism while giving advice. Dr. Bai has treated many people with great success including simple ordinary people to a psychiatrist and other doctors. These people sought help elsewhere without results. Dr. Bai is exceptionally talented in applying acupuncture and massage.

Her ability in dealing with people is not measurable but satisfactory and comforting. She is so thoughtful and generous, bringing me food I love and well as fresh organic herbs from her garden. She also gives me good financial advice. Recently she treated me to dinner at a Chinese Restaurant on my birthday and brought home leftovers to enjoy the next day. I am so extremely indebted to her. How fortunate I am! Everyone should be so lucky!

Dr. Dongfeng Sun

Dr. Dongfeng Sun was born in China. His family immigrated to Canada in 1997. He has studied medicine for 10 years in 3 medical schools and has an additional 8 years of clinical medical practice experience in China. Dr. Sun has ample experience in general primary medical care, along with familiarity in the intensive care unit. He also has experience working in the emergency room during his six years of residency training and two years experience as an in charge physician in Cardiology. He passed the MCCEE and MCCQE for Canadian medical license application tests after he moved to Canada. Now, Dr. Sun practices as a registered clinical assistant at Leukemia and Bone Marrow Transplant Unit at Health Sciences Center in Winnipeg.

Dr. Sun has a great experience in medical research. His Doctorate Degree project was in atherosclerosis research, which study was focused on the role of fibrinolytic factors in the development of atherosclerosis. With his supervisor, Dr. Junren Zhu and his colleagues, he authored and co-authored four papers in prestigious scientific journals in China. To learn more advanced research approaches, after he graduated from Shanghai Medical University in 1996, he consciously exposed himself to different research environments at the University of Manitoba. He worked on diabetes, allergy as well as liver diseases research. In his post-doctoral training in Dr. Estelle Simons' laboratory at the University of Manitoba, he studied deeply the molecular pathogenesis of mosquito allergy focusing on the mechanism in the development of sensitization and desensitization to mosquito bite. (See International Immunology, 2001; 12:1445-1452 and Canadian Journal of Allergy and Clinical Immunology, 2002; 7:34-40)

From July 1999 to June 2008, Dr. Sun worked at Dr. Gerald Minuk's laboratory in the Hepatology Section, University of Manitoba and engaged in the project to study the role of GABAergic activity in the process of hepatocellular carcinoma development. This work was published in Am J Pysiol Gastrointest Liver Physiol 2003; 285: G12-G19. They also investigated the occult hepatitis B virus infection in North American population. Their research has been published in Hepatology 2004; 40:1072-1077 and Journal of Hepatology 2005; 42: 480-485.

Hon Stephen Harper

You, Prime Minister Harper are best suited for "A Vision of Canada in 2020: How to Save Canadian Medicare and Money." Canadians have reelected you as Prime Minister with a minority – your followers are very dedicated and faithful. That minority government will change to a majority if you follow my plan. You will make dramatic changes in your strategy by using your intuition and your analytical mind that will drastically affect your standing, both at home and abroad.

Doctor of Canadian Medical Association

You will be the most famous and influential person this country has ever had. You will be admired and revered both at home and abroad because you will have solved the obesity epidemic. You will introduce a diet program going back to the beginning (prior to the introduction of the food industry – the cause of obesity). You will be instrumental in devising a "back-to-the-earth food diet, which will not only nourish the body but will prevent diseases like cancer, etc. You will be sought after by people all over the world. Your name will evoke a fame unequalled or enjoyed by any other person. And little wonder when you can solve the obesity epidemic and self/healing/ preventing diseases. You will also use an ancient Chinese method called "Ayurveda". A science of restoring balance using herbs, diet, lifestyle, yoga, Vedic astrology, energy points, aroma therapy, gem stones, Vastu Shasta (similar to Feng Shui) and various other therapeutic means to promote (Sukham) well-being. The ultimate goal is that China, India and Canada will form an alliance to promote ultimate health habits and to live by "Art of Living" discipline.

President Hu Jintao

Hu Jintao (born 21 December 1942) is currently the Paramount Leader of the People's Republic of China, holding the titles of General Secretary of the Communist Party of China since 2002, President of the People's Republic of China since 2003, and Chairman of the Central Military Commission since 2004, succeeding Jiang Zemin in the fourth generation leadership of the People's Republic of China. Since his ascendancy, Hu has reinstated certain controls on the economy and has been largely conservative with political reforms. His foreign policy is seen as less conciliatory than that of his predecessor, though China's global influence has increased while he has been in office.

Hu's rise to the presidency represents China's transition of leadership from old, establishment Communists to younger, more pragmatic technocrats. For most of Hu's adult life he has been involved in the Communist party bureaucracy, notably as Party Chief for the Tibet Autonomous Region, and then later Vice-President under Jiang Zemin. An advocate for China's peaceful rise, Hu's political philosophy is summarily described as aiming to found a basis for a *Harmonious Society* domestically and for *Peaceful Development* internationally, the former generated by a Scientific Development Concept, which seeks integrated solutions to tackle China's various economic, environmental and social problems.

Prime Minister Manmohan Singh

Manmohan Singh (born 26 September 1932) is the 17th and current Prime Minister of India. An economist by profession, Dr. Singh worked at organizations like the International Monetary Fund and the United Nations. From 1982 to 1985, he was the governor of the Reserve Bank of India. Singh is a member of the Indian National Congress party, and became the first Sikh Prime Minister of India on 22 May 2004. He is considered one of the most influential figures in India's recent history, mainly because of the Economic Reforms he had initiated in 1991 when he was Finance Minister under Prime Minister Narasimha Rao.

Celine Dion

Ms Dion is the most important Canadian singer because having come from a humble background she has reached super stardom with a voice un-matched in this world. She is very special to Canadians because she is a French-Canadian, which is our bilingual heritage. When she sings "O Canada" in French or

English or a combination of both, it is a breath stopper and a tear jerker for every Canadian who hears it. We are so fortunate to have such a great Canadian that brings joy to every person in the world.

Honorable John Ralston Saul

He has argued that Canada is a Métis nation, heavily influenced and shaped by aboriginal ideas. Our roots are in the oldest culture of Canada's Seven Sacred Teachings and the Addictions Healing Circles (by Elder Larry Monkman). John Ralston Saul maintains that in order to prevent extinction we need to incorporate aboriginal languages in our culture. It is only through language that we can express ourselves as individuals and as a group. He also maintains that our waterways are our highways or roads leading to our destination and gives us the right to sovereignty – that's a given.

Michael J Fox

Michael J. Fox (born Michael Andrew Fox; June 9, 1961) is a Canadian-born American actor. His roles include Marty McFly from the Back to the Future trilogy (1985–1990); Alex P. Keaton from Family Ties (1982–1989), for which he won three Emmy Awards and a Golden Globe Award; and Mike Flaherty from Spin City (1996–2000), for which he won an Emmy, three Golden Globes, and two Screen Actors Guild Awards.

Fox was diagnosed with Parkinson's disease in 1991, and disclosed his condition to the public in 1998. As the symptoms of his disease worsened, he semi-retired from acting in 2000.

Fox married actress Tracy Pollan on July 16, 1988, at West Mountain Inn in Arlington, VT. The couple have four children: Sam Michael (born May 30, 1989), twins Aquinnah Kathleen and Schuyler Frances (born February 15, 1995), and Esmé

Annabelle (born November 3, 2001). Fox holds dual Canadian-U.S. citizenship.

Fox started displaying symptoms of early-onset Parkinson's disease in 1990 while shooting the movie Doc Hollywood, though he wasn't properly diagnosed until the next year. In 1998, he decided to go public with his condition, and since then he has been a strong advocate of Parkinson's disease research. His foundation, The Michael J. Fox Foundation, was created to help advance Parkinson's disease research through embryonic stem cell studies.

One of the few people to know that Fox had Parkinson's Disease before 1998 was one of Michael's best friends, his stunt double Charles Croughwell on Doc Hollywood. In later years, he and Fox developed a system of hiding Michael's symptoms.

Fox, in a 2006 interview with Katie Couric, explained his political advocacy, "I'm in this situation with millions of other Americans... and we have a right, if there are answers out there, to pursue those answers with the full support of our politicians".

Two years earlier, Fox had appeared in a television commercial for Republican Arlen Specter's 2004 Senate campaign. In the commercial, sponsored by Specter's re-election campaign, Fox comments that Specter "gets it" and Specter's voice is heard saying, "There is hope."

On July 18, 2006, Fox appeared in a taped interview on ABC's Good Morning America, defending a Senate bill (Stem Cell Research Enhancement Act) that would have expanded federal funding for stem cell research. The bill was not enacted, however, being vetoed by President George W. Bush.

For the November 2006 U.S. midterm elections, Fox endorsed candidates on the basis of their support of embryonic stem cell research, as different from adult stem cell research. He appeared at events for several candidates including New Jersey Senator Bob Menendez, Iowa Secretary of State and gubernatorial candidate Chet Culver, Illinois congressional candidate Tammy Duckworth, Virginia senatorial candidate James Webb and Ohio senatorial candidate Congressman Sherrod Brown.

In late October 2006, Fox appeared in a television campaign commercial, endorsing Claire McCaskill, the Democratic candidate for U.S. Senate in Missouri and opposing incumbent senator Jim Talent for his specific opposition to federal funding of embryonic stem cell research. Fox also made similar ads in Wisconsin (supporting Governor Jim Doyle) and in Maryland, endorsing senatorial candidate Congressman Ben Cardin. All three of the endorsed politicians won their respective elections.

Conservative radio talk show host Rush Limbaugh caused controversy by claiming Michael J. Fox was "either off his medication or he was acting." Limbaugh later said he would apologize to Fox "if I am wrong in characterizing his behavior on this commercial as an act. . ." Elaine Richman, a neuroscientist in Baltimore who co-wrote <u>Parkinson's disease and the Family</u> offered the opinion that "Anyone who knows the disease well would regard his movement as classic severe Parkinson's disease. Any other interpretation is misinformed."

Fox responded to Limbaugh's comments, "... it's difficult for people who don't have Parkinson's, or don't know about Parkinson's, to understand the symptoms and the way they work and the way medication works. You get what you get on any given day".

Parkinson's disease (PD) is a chronic neurological disorder which can be characterized by four cardinal symptoms: rigidity (specifically "leadpipe" and "cogwheeling" rigidity), resting tremor, postural instability, and bradykinesia (slow movement). At present, there is no cure, but medications provide some relief from the symptoms. Fox manages his symptoms using Sinemet, a commercial form of Levodopa (L-DOPA) and carbidopa. L-DOPA treatment decreases in effectiveness as it is used over a long period of time, so Fox, like many PD sufferers, extends the life of its effectiveness by using it as little as possible.

In his memoir, <u>Lucky Man</u>, Fox wrote that he did not take his medication prior to his testimony before the Senate Appropriations Subcommittee in 1998. "I had made a deliberate choice to appear before the subcommittee without medication. It seemed to me that this occasion demanded that my testimony about the effects of the disease, and the urgency we as a community were feeling, be seen as well as heard. For people who had never observed me in this kind of shape, the transformation must have been startling."

David Northcott

David Northcott is Executive Director of Winnipeg Harvest.

In a recent article entitled: "Too many Manitobans have Empty Bowls", he wrote:

"For 25 years our doors have been open at Winnipeg Harvest. We await the day when we will be able to close them. Unfortunately, the need is still there for us to provide hungry in Manitoba. With last year's 18% increase in food bank use in Manitoba; the highest on record, it doesn't look promising. There were 48,000 Manitobans using our services last year. A disturbing fact was almost half of those recipients were children.

More than ever, Winnipeg Harvest needs your support. We want to give those we share food with a hand up. With disproportionate number of children receiving food from us, isn't it time to look at a human rights platform for responding to this growing concern? With over half of our recipients receiving social assistance, isn't it time to look at a refundable family tax benefit. Human rights and the right to food should be basis of engagement of issues in any civil society.

With the recent Ombudsman report that addressed 68 points dealing with poverty, it's an outline for action. We need to keep working with government to affect change while walking alongside families to give them support they need for a food secure home.

As much as anyone, we are hopeful of a recovery in both Canadian and Global economy; living wage jobs and strengthening of our social safety net. All are assets for all Canadians.

Winnipeg Harvest's Empty Bowls Program and fundraising activities – including Empty Bowls in the Schools, Empty Bowls Souper Lunch at MTS Centre, October 26, 11am-2pm and the amazing Empty Bowls Celebrity Auction, November 10, Delta Winnipeg – not only raise vulnerable funds for Winnipeg Harvest, but create awareness of issues of hunger and poverty in Manitoba.

Please join us and make your donation to the Empty Bowls program today. Learn more by calling 982-FOOD or donate online at www.winnipegharvest.org "

See also Appendix II for his presentation to the Senate subcommittee on Cities, May 1, 2008.

The Flin Flon Miners:

The contributions of the Flin Flon Miners to Manitoba and to the whole country are well documented.

Among the more prominent Flin Floners are:

Rod McIsaaac Sr

Jack Freed man

Joe Prendville

<u>Frank Dembinsky</u>

<u>David Collins:</u> Local Trapper

<u>Tom Creighton:</u> Prospector (1914) – Novel "Flintabatly Flonatin" – from which Flin Flon got its name.

Joe Brain

The Joe Brain Foundation Inc. is a private Canadian foundation which provides small grants to Manitoba based registered charitable organizations. Joe was my husband Clarence Hannaford's friend because Clarence supplied him with unemployment insurance benefits which enabled him to buy food while he was prospecting. He gets credit for discovering Hanson Lake mine, the first commercial mine at Hanson Lake - rich deposit of zinc, lead, and silver. Consequently we shared in the profits with the three others when the discovery was sold. After Clarence died, I received a payment and was able to send Rod, my son, to the University of Kingston (Military) where he was accepted because of his high high-school marks and his determination to save money and become successful financially and he did, in computer software (SAP) founded in Germany. Rod introduced SAP it into Canada in Ottawa and Toronto, then into the United Sates. Being an "unknown" , he was forced to join forces with Deloitte and Touche and as a result received less profit.

Lew Parres

Developed the idea of mid Canada corridor, a huge mountain of ice covering a large area of central Canada, moving down slowly and making its way down North America. A unique concept of ice age activity.

Thompson Brothers

Whose parents forbad them to marry. If they did they would lose their inheritance. The older two bothers and the two sisters lived in their parent's old home in Cranberry-Portage where they entertained at "tea" using an English tea wagon.

Helen Chance, David Hannaford's birth mother, worked for the Thompson brothers and knew their names. One of them didn't stay single but married or lived with his girlfriend in an exclusive part of Toronto. He did well in his investments in mining and became very wealthy.

The Richardson Family

A financial company in Winnipeg, Manitoba invested in the mine industry and invited the two Thompson brothers and their two sisters to be their guests at their home in Winnipeg. The sisters were still wearing their old clothes from way back including old aviator caps discounted from war-time use. The attire of the brothers was acceptable but not the sisters. So the boys ordered formal gowns to be made or bought at Mary-Jane Shop in Flin Flon and had the trunk of the sisters' old clothes (included), destroyed.

The Whitney Family

Owners of the Hudson Bay Mining and Smelting. Smoke pollution is a problem. Also cooling ore resulted in tragic death of employees. Safety of employees is a current issue. (Flin Flon Miner paper and the Freepress letters to the Editor).

CHAPTER II:
HEROS AND VISIONARIES

INDIA - HEROES

Canada recognizes and gives thanks to Mahatma Ghandi for his vision and practice of peaceful protest. He devoted his life to showing the world how to live by peaceful means not by military power. He did this single handedly! Mahatma Ghandi's contribution and dedication is embedded in the world and will remain, never to be forgotten - Another Great Hero! Mother Theresa has inspired others to help by her example.

SRI SRI RAVI-SHANKAR - HERO

More than any other person on earth Canadians and the rest of the world are blessed and honored by the presence and practice of HIS HOLINESS RAVI-SHANKAR. His Art of Living (AOL) organization is worldwide and incomparable. AOL is a vast foundation and has centers in more than 140 countries including Canada. They are located from coast to coast not only in major cities but also in many smaller cities as follows; Halifax, Montreal, Quebec City, Trois-Rivieres, Sherbrook, Grandby, Ottawa, Toronto, Kingston, Mississauga, Brampton, London, Windsor, Waterloo, Sarnia, York Region, Winnipeg, Regina,

Calgary, Edmonton, Vancouver, Victoria and Surrey. Notable are the number of AOL (Five) in Quebec. Art of Living Foundation Head Quarters is located there.

AOL offers a variety of courses and is influential and effective internally and externally. These can be found in the book "Guru of Joy" by Francois Gautier from pages 263 to 269.

SRI SRI, now referred to as Guruji, possesses unsurpassed qualities. He has a phenomenal memory. He never forgets a name or a face. He speaks several languages. His every word has significance. His mind is like a computer, extremely analytical, yet tireless. He is also phenomenally intuitive. He can fathom the content of a book by reading only a few lines, know exactly, by what state of consciousness you are in by giving you one glance, He can assess a situation by sensing it in a few seconds. Page 118 from "The Guru of Joy"

Children are attracted to Him like the Pied Piper. Guruji is lots of fun. Entertainment activities can also be found in the book. "Laugh and make others laugh; don't get entangled and don't entangle others" is amongst his most popular quotes.

Some people ask Guruji why He doesn't take a more active part in solving current social problems, wars, terrorism, crime, sickness and dissension. This can be found in the book under 5H Program. Canadians, like many other people in the world, know why - because it doesn't work. They know Guruji knows best. He starts making changes or reform by beginning with the individual "from the roots upward" thus insuring a strong and secure start. Then comes the family and the community, people working together and helping each other get rid of their problems and having a chance in life to realize their full potential as human beings with compassion, generosity, caring, non-violence, harmony, respect and realization of their oneness with nature - the elements air, water, minerals, earth, plants, animals - that they abide by the rules of nature (or creator) given to them to enjoy, not abuse - for these things are not independent - each making a contribution - combining together to form a "oneness" with all the earth. Refer to the book <u>Guru of Joy</u> by Francois Gautier for more information. Sri Sri Ravi Shankar feels that ending violence in society is one of the greatest challenges in today's world. All forms of violence including youth violence, domestic violence, human rights violations, criminal behavior and war - spring from the same seed of hatred. How can hatred be eliminated? Look for these answers in the book <u>Guru of Joy</u> by Francois Gautier (pp.158-159).

How to accomplish world peace and harmony depends on the participation of Sri Sri's AOL program. It is essential for developing techniques that remove stress, giving a sense of well being and peace of mind and of having a vibrant feeling for life, a euphoric state of mind. The courses offered are progressive, leading many to advanced courses that make you realize that the AOL well is really all about letting go, dropping your expectations and your hang-ups and realizing how Sri Sri takes you step by step. Please refer to the book <u>Guru of Joy</u> by Francois Gautier for more information on page 155.

One of the goals of this book is to reveal the Art of Living Foundation for its healing powers and making this a better and happier world for everyone and everything in it. Canadians are appealing to philanthropists the world over to invest in the establishment of many more Art of Living Foundation locations with FREE access. What better way to leave a legacy that continues to bring peace and happiness and spreads to every corner of the earth. That's Canada's sincere wish.

Each master is an expression of Infinity, as is our consciousness. The human mind cannot comprehend infinity and likewise cannot comprehend the Divine. Sri Sri is both mystic and worldly.

People that participate in the AOL programs will be aware that they must spare Sri Sri in order to protect Him from Himself. They will do His work so He will live for many, many years.

That is Canada's sincere wish.

NORTH AMERICAN – HERO

Martin Luther King, Jr. (January 15, 1929 – April 4, 1968)

An American clergyman, activist and prominent leader in the African-American civil rights movement. His main legacy was to secure progress on civil rights in the United States and he is frequently referenced as a human rights icon today.

ABORIGINAL PEOPLE OF CANADA - HEROES

A Salute to Aboriginals for their Contributions.

Canadians will treat Aboriginal people with the greatest respect. They will recognize for the first time that these are the people who are the First Canadians and all others are secondary. Aboriginals are victims of countless betrayals and horrendous suffering. Canadians will join hands with aboriginals to help them recover from their losses and from their years of pain inflicted by foreigners.

From the time Canada was first invaded and conquered by foreigners, aboriginals became victims of genocide and disease. Foreigners established Reserves (Concentration Camps) where they mixed tribes unfriendly to each other in order to create dissension. This tactic was used to destroy each tribe's culture and language so they could be integrated and assimilated into the foreign society. Another method of assimilation that was used was to break up families. Children were taken away from their parents and placed in Christian Religion Schools run by priests and nuns. Children at these schools were beaten if they spoke their own language. They were not able to console each other for fear of being caught and beaten as a result. If a child wet his or her bed some nuns rubbed that child's nose in the urine as a punishment and the child was made to wash the bedding by hand. Frustrated nuns took their frustration out on innocent aboriginal children beating them severely. These young aboriginal children had not broken any rules yet they were badly beaten to satisfy the sick needs of some nuns. Canadians will face the truth and the shame that their forebears bestowed on the Aboriginals. Like the Bible says "the sons of the fathers will bear the fruits of their doing." Canadians will be bearing those fruits to try to make amends by joining all aboriginals as partners. Many children were sexually abused by priests. They were threatened with severe punishment if they revealed the abuse. The suffering was and is indescribable - extremely deep-rooted and not relievable - a lifetime of guilt and shame. Some babies born to nuns on the premises were buried secretly in the basement (secret cemetery). Bones of these babies were discovered revealing this unbelievably horrifying disregard for human life.

As a result of their experience in the Christian Schools aboriginal people have turned to use of drugs and violence to combat the pain they feel. That has led to views of aboriginals by white Canadians as no good, useless and a drain on government funding by way of compensation. Many Canadians resent the compensation. They say that aboriginals get 'everything' free. They resent for example that aboriginals get taxis for transportation and food vouchers, all at government expense. They view these and others as advantages they don't get, making them feel antagonistic toward all aboriginals. Results of racial slurs like 'the only good Indian is a dead one' is repeated with relish and a sense of authority and ridicule.

Culture and Civilization

Foreigners who invaded North America viewed the aboriginal

people as uncivilized, backward, with pagan beliefs that were simply imaginary (without reality) or of any use. They did not consider that in spite of their views these same people helped them survive starvation, scurvy and many other illnesses.

Practice of Sharing

Aboriginals have a unique, kind and considerate way of taking care of each other. They share with each other whenever there is a need, ensuring that in doing so they will be taken care of if and when they may be in the same situation. This aspect of their culture and ideology is the source of their helping the foreigners survive. Aboriginal cultures' philosophy is based on a theory that you do not take more that you need, so that when aboriginals were employed, they would stop working when they felt that their needs were fulfilled. This lead to the misperception by the establishment that they were lazy. This was not the case, they weren't being greedy and working for a profit. Once they stopped working it allowed them free time to spend with their relatives to exchange ideas and pass on knowledge.

They used pemmican to provide nutrition and to prevent scurvy. They dried fish, berries, and many herbs (like Seneca Root) for winter use as food when fresh food was unavailable. Theirs was a highly organized culture based on ideology, ecological practice and ceremony. Their ideology is the concept of an interdependence of all things on earth. A hierarchy of importance begins with Man and ends with the Great Spirit Manitou. The hierarchy is in the following order of dependency; man, animals, plants, elements (sunshine, air, wind, water, rocks, minerals and earth) and at the top, the Great Spirit Creator Manitou.

Aboriginal civilization practiced ecology by burning old trees to get new growth, sustaining a strong environment. Water was diverted to prevent flooding and erosion. Crops of maize, tubers etc were planted between, and with complimentary plants.

Alternate places were used giving each a chance to recover from use and to rebuild the soil content.

A medicine man "Shaman" gave spiritual advice and prayer to the Great Spirit in appreciation of all the blessings bestowed upon the people by all of the things on the planet.

Color, Directions and Feathers are important symbols to the aboriginal culture.

Animals and Birds play a very important and significant role in the aboriginal culture. These are viewed as essential partners or friends, providing food and protection against disease or danger. There is no fear of endangered species because ecological practice is built into the aboriginal culture. These concepts are results of great depth of analysis and experience.

Ceremonial Activities

Rain Dance speaks to the elements and "Manitou" for help in providing rain during needy times.

Dancing and Singing with special sacred drum, invokes the spirit world and helps with personal problems.

Throat Singing is a unique way of defining who they are and provides a rare experience for the listener.

Potlatch Ceremony is a concept of a chief giving away all his material acquisitions each year. If he can acquire more goods than any other competitor he will justifiably retain his position as leader and chief. A very unique way of re-electing your leader.

Hopi Kachinas (or Katsinas) dolls are actually stylized religious icons, meticulously carved from cottonwood root and painted to represent figures from Hopi mythology. For generations, these figures have been used to teach children about their religion. Authentic Kachina dolls are made only by Hopi artists. Genuine

Kachina dolls are made by only a small number of Hopi carvers who have dedicated their lives to this art--it takes years of practice and religious study to master Kachina carving.

Medicine

Aboriginal use of herbs for health problems, was instrumental in developing modern day medicine.

Development Of Arts

Aboriginal people made pottery by hand using different kinds of clay. These pieces were used for different things, like dry storage, water storage, cooking and display. These are very unique in composition and require analytical knowledge to produce.

Weaving - they used homemade dyes to make colorful pieces for different purposes - some for clothing, some for different kinds of covers, others for display. The weavers competed with each other to see who could make the finest, resulting in a very high quality product. These are worthy of museum display and of great value. They took such great pride in their work! Shells, seeds, porcupine needles, colorful stones, feathers etc were used as decorations for clothing, necklaces, etc and for other adornment and for display. They were unequaled artists of great admirations and accomplishment!

Biting Birch bark - A rare gift of depicting a scene of an image of recognition. It's not practiced in any other culture and is at risk because very few are continuing to learn this art.

Inuit Culture

The Inuit is an equally valued Aboriginal Culture of Canada that teaches us how to adjust and live in harmony with our environment. The Inuit consume a lot of whale fat when available. If and when it is not available they will not starve to death because their body will feed itself from their stored body fat.

When dying, Inuit have a custom of remaining alone so those who accompanied the dying person will not be at risk in returning home. It's a wonderful last deed in contribution to save other lives.

Sex is a natural uninhibited occasion for joy and laughter which Inuit women are generous to share. There is no perversion or Victorian taboo or suffering from guilt or fear or stress but a wonderful therapy.

Babies are welcome and are cradled on their mothers back using soft moss as diapering, easy to dispose of and replace with fresh.

Snow

The Inuit have different words to describe different types of snow suitable for certain uses. Their construction of igloos requires knowledge of scientific degree. Inside the igloo, the placing of sleeping quarters, cooking stones and utensils are strategic. All the things they use from sleighs to cutting knives (different kinds are used for different tasks) are all made from the local environment or from another locality.

Soapstone Carving - This is a wonderful way of recording their cultural activities. There was admiration for fine carving and each carver strove to improve his skill. Birds, fish and bears were depicted sometimes with human parts conveying their close relationships and interdependency. More recent carvings are specialized depicting the American eagle, geese, loons, walrus etc. The highly talented people of the Inuit culture deserve our deepest respect and admiration.

This Inuit aboriginal culture was capable of so many developments, original, innovative, organized and creative, was looked upon by foreigners as uncivilized, ignorant, lacking of any concept of a real society! En-lighted by their own technology of weapons and other destructive means, foreigners saw their methods of killing and destroying versus saving lives and helping as being superior. Canadians feel empathy towards the aboriginals. They will rid our nation of past superiority attitudes. The shoe is now on the other foot.

Tom Ford - Managing editor of The Issues Network - The Winnipeg Free Press

Pierre Trudeau the late prime minister is quoted as saying, "all of us feel a sense of guilt, not so much towards the Indian, as to the fact that we haven't really addressed the problem." Mike Maunder a Winnipeg adviser on inner-city life captures a preconception of our general society. The aboriginals have a problem, and we - the non-aboriginals - have to take the initiative to solve it. Only if these assumptions can be transcended, says Maunder, can all Canadians undo the system of relationships that now exists and allow something new to emerge. Improving educational systems will mean that more aboriginals will be able to make a "free choice about where they live," unencumbered by a lack of knowledge about their culture, life outside a reserve, or the skills needed to get a job in contemporary society. Canada needs aboriginal workers. "In the race of life, many aboriginals start well back of the starting line," Says former Prime Minister Paul Martin, who has been studying aboriginal issues. A recent study, Martin adds, "found that aboriginals who do have a high school diploma tend to find jobs that not only equal, but can exceed the success ratios of other Canadians." In the election campaign two years ago Prime Minister Stephen Harper said Conservative government would have a "fundamental obligation" to improve "the educational and economic opportunities of all aboriginal Canadians."

On June 16, 2008, Prime Minister Harper, on behalf of all Canadians apologized for the harm and suffering that Aboriginals endured and still endure. He promised to make amends by settling land claims and personal claims. As a result, Canadians will experience far-reaching implications. The guilt and shame will be punishment for remaining silent when children were being abused under the guise of assimilation.

On behalf of all Aboriginals, Grand Chief Phil Fontaine, graciously accepted the apology. He said it helped to begin the healing so badly needed. Native people in attendance cried with relief. Phil Fontaine and Judge Simpson were child victims of abuse.

Canadians will introduce new school programs into the curriculum to educate new generations. They need to know the history and the truth. This has also opened the door to other cultural abuses by the Canadian government. The Chinese, Japanese, Ukrainian, and German groups of people were victims of wartime abuse. In addition, unemployed Canadians were victims of abuse, shot at by the establishment in Winnipeg during the Winnipeg Strike of 1919.

The Canadian record of cultural genocide and abuse is shameful. Canadians must admit their wrongdoing before any healing can take place. For once and for all, Canadians must expose the truth about their misdeeds and must ask forgiveness of themselves. They must forgive their offenders. Only by forgiveness will true relief become a reality.

VISIONARIES

Her Excellency The Right Honorable Michaëlle Jean

Jean is Canada's first Governor General of Caribbean origin; the third woman (after Jeanne Sauvé and Adrienne Clarkson); the fourth youngest (after The Marquees of Lorne, who was 33 years old in 1878; The Marquis of Lansdowne, who was 38 years old in 1883; and Edward Schreyer, who was 43 years old in 1979); the fourth former journalist (after Sauvé, Roméo LeBlanc and Clarkson); and the second after Clarkson to not only have neither a political nor military background, but also to be a visible minority, to break the tradition of Canadian-born Governors General, and to be in an interracial marriage. Jean is also the first representative of Queen Elizabeth II to have been born during the latter's reign, and her appointment saw the first child living in Rideau Hall since Schreyer and his young family lived there in the early 1980s.

Jean is a refugee from Haiti — coming to Canada in 1968 — and was raised in the town of Thetford Mines, Quebec. After receiving a number of university degrees, Jean worked as a journalist and broadcaster for Radio-Canada and the Canadian Broadcasting Corporation (CBC), as well as undertaking charity work, mostly in the field of assisting victims of domestic violence. Her participation in some of the film works by her husband, Jean-Daniel Lafond, through the 1990s, as well as her holding of French citizenship, later caused controversy when her appointment as Governor General was publicized; recorded comments of hers were construed by some as favouring Quebec sovereignty, and her dual citizenship caused doubt about her loyalties. Jean denied separatist leanings and renounced her citizenship of France.

Jean focused strongly on the plight of female victims of violence, meeting with representatives of women's organizations during foreign visits, as well as during her visits to Canada's provinces.

Awards

- **1989**: the Human Rights League of Canada Media Award
- **1989**: *Foundation Mireille Lanctôt Prix Mireille-Lanctôt*
- **1994**: Canadian Broadcasting Corporation Prix Anik
- **1995**: Amnesty International Canada Journalism Award
- **1997**: City of Montreal Citizen of Honor
- **2000**: *Conseil de la Langue Française du Québec Prix Raymond-Charette*
- **2000**: Canadian Association of Cable Television Providers Galaxy Award

- **2001**: Academy of Canadian Cinema and Television Gemini Award
- **2003**: *Chevalier du l'Ordre de la Pléiade de l'Association des parlementaires de langue française*
- **2004**: Canadian Broadcasting Corporation French Television Prize
- **16 November 2009**: National Quality Institute Recognition of Achievement Awards

Foreign honors

1985: Swiss Ambassador to Canada's Prize of Excellence in French and Italian studies

Condolences:

An unprecedented response to Haiti's devastating earthquake led to teaching the world how to achieve a common goal by cooperating (friend and foe) for the common good of all. This is an age of philanthropy that is phenomenally widespread and unknown in the past. It has touched the hearts from individuals to families, to school rooms, offices, places at work, clubs, multi residential buildings, colleges, universities, hospitals, and many other institutions and business places to communities, cities, countries and the whole world. Of course it is emotionally inspired, so what? As long as it achieves its goal of starting a new way of living.

Let us give up wars and killing each other and learn from the people of Haiti who died that there is another way to live. And that they did not die in vain. Never before has there been this joining of hands worldwide by individuals to help those in need. Haitians who gave up their lives taught the Art of Living.

Many other problems on this earth are equally solvable by philanthropic donations. Ending rape warfare in Africa and rebuilding that country into a self sustaining safe place where people help each other is only one example of many what Haitians have taught.

It is a time when Haiti's political stance is neither questioned nor even considered, which shows how little politics count at a time of disaster.

Our deepest condolences to Her Excellency Michaëlle Jean and her family and all Haitians who lost their loved ones in this unprecedented disaster. Everyone is vulnerable.

We are proud and appreciative and we thank you Madam Jean, you are our heroine!

"We shall overcome - We shall overcome-We shall overcome someday"

Michael Moore

Michael Francis Moore (born April 23, 1954) is an American filmmaker, author and liberal political commentator. He is the director and producer of *Bowling for Columbine*, *Fahrenheit 9/11*, *Sicko*, and *Capitalism: A Love Story*, four of the top eight highest-grossing documentaries of all time. In September 2008, he released his first free movie on the Internet, *Slacker Uprising*, documenting his personal crusade to encourage more Americans to vote in presidential elections. He has also written and starred in the TV shows *TV Nation* and *The Awful Truth*.

Moore is a self-described liberal who has criticized globalization, large corporations, assault weapon ownership, the Iraq War, U.S. President George W. Bush and the American health care system in his written and cinematic works.

Directing/producing

Roger & Me

Moore first became famous for his 1989 film, *Roger & Me,* a documentary about what happened to Flint, Michigan after General Motors closed its factories and opened new ones in Mexico, where the workers were paid much less. Since then Moore has been known as a critic of the neoliberal view of globalization. "Roger" is Roger B. Smith, former CEO and president of General Motors.

Pets or Meat: The Return to Flint

(1992) is a short (23-minute) documentary film that was aired on PBS. It is based on the feature-length film *Roger & Me* (1989) by Michael Moore.

Canadian Bacon

In 1995, Moore released a satirical film, *Canadian Bacon,* which features a fictional US president (played by Alan Alda) engineering a fake war with Canada in order to boost his popularity. It is noted for containing a number of Canadian and American stereotypes, and for being Moore's only non-documentary film.

The Big One

In 1997, Moore directed *The Big One,* which documents the tour publicizing his book *Downsize This! Random Threats from an Unarmed American,* in which he criticizes mass layoffs despite record corporate profits. Among others, he targets Nike for outsourcing shoe production to Indonesia.

Bowling for Columbine

Moore's 2002 film, *Bowling for Columbine,* probes the culture of guns and violence in the United States, taking as a starting point the Columbine High School massacre of 1999. *Bowling for*

Columbine won the Anniversary Prize at the 2002 Cannes Film Festival and France's Cesar Award as the Best Foreign Film.

Fahrenheit 9/11

Fahrenheit 9/11 examines America in the aftermath of the September 11, 2001 attacks, particularly the record of the Bush administration and alleged links between the families of George W. Bush and Osama bin Laden. *Fahrenheit* was awarded the *Palme d'Or*, the top honor at the 2004 Cannes Film Festival; it was the first documentary film to win the prize since 1956.

Sicko

Moore directed this film about the American health care system, focusing particularly on the managed-care and pharmaceutical industries. At least four major pharmaceutical companies—Pfizer, Eli Lilly, AstraZeneca, and GlaxoSmithKline—ordered their employees not to grant any interviews to Moore. According to Moore on a letter at his website, "roads that often surprise us and lead us to new ideas – and challenge us to reconsider the ones we began with have caused some minor delays."

Captain Mike Across America

Moore takes a look at the politics of college students in what he calls "Bush Administration America" with this film shot during Moore's 60-city college campus tour in the months leading up to the 2004 election. The film was later re-edited by Moore into *Slacker Uprising*.

Capitalism: A Love Story

On September 23, 2009, Moore released a new movie titled *Capitalism: A Love Story*, which looks at the financial crisis of 2007–2010 and the U.S. economy during the transition between the incoming Obama Administration and the outgoing Bush Administration.

Filmography

- *Roger & Me* (1989)
- *Pets or Meat: The Return to Flint* (1992) (TV)
- *Canadian Bacon* (1995)
- *The Big One* (1997)
- *And Justice for All* (1998) (TV)
- *Lucky Numbers* (2000) (as actor)
- *Bowling for Columbine* (2002)
- *Fahrenheit 9/11* (2004) "Palme d'Or" in Cannes
- *Sicko* (2007)
- *Captain Mike Across America* (2007)
- *Slacker Uprising* (2008)
- *Capitalism: A Love Story* (2009)

Television

- *TV Nation* (1994)
- *The Awful Truth* (1999)
- *Michael Moore Live (1999)*

You are a modern Pete Seeger who gave hope and help to the disadvantaged and the desperate during The Great Depression. You are now fulfilling Pete Seeger's "shoes/dreams". How fortunate we are to have you and to know that you will continue to be on our side in our struggle for equality! I thank you with all my heart for all the work that you have done & hope you will continue.

Daniel Tammet

Daniel Paul Tammet (born 31 January 1979) is a British high-functioning autistic savant gifted with a facility for mathematical and natural language learning. He was born Daniel Corney (later deciding to change his surname to Tammet), the first of nine children, to working-class parents in London. In his memoir, <u>Born on a Blue Day</u>, he talks about how having epilepsy, synaesthesia, and Asperger Syndrome all deeply affected his childhood.

In 2006, Tammet traveled to the United States to promote his memoir, <u>Born on a Blue Day</u>: <u>Inside the Extraordinary Mind of an Autistic Savant</u>. Tammet was born on a Wednesday, a day he perceives as the color blue. While on his U.S. book tour, he appeared on several television and radio talk shows and specials, including 60 Minutes and David Letterman's Late Show. In February 2007 <u>Born on a Blue Day</u> was serialized as BBC Radio 4's Book of the Week in the United Kingdom. He describes his meeting with Kim Peek, upon whom Rain Man was based, as one of the happiest moments of his life. They connected when they asked each other date calculations based on their birth dates, and got the correct answers instantly.

Tammet's new book <u>Embracing the Wide Sky</u>, attempts to shed light on the mystery of savants' mental abilities. Tammet argues that the differences between savant and non-savant minds have been exaggerated.

Jimmy Carter

James Earl Carter, Jr. was born in the small farming town of Plains, Georgia. His father, James Earl Carter, Sr., known as Earl, was a farmer and businessman. His mother, Lillian Gordy, was a registered nurse. When Jimmy Carter was four years old, the family moved to a farm in the nearby community of Archery. Jimmy Carter has described the world of his childhood movingly in his 2001 book, <u>An Hour Before Daylight: Memoirs of a Rural Boyhood</u>. Although the Carter family home lacked both electricity and running water, the Carters were one of the more prosperous families in the community. Most of their neighbors, and young Jimmy's playmates in Archery, were African American, but the rigid code of segregation required the separation of the races in school, in church and other public places. Carter's mother, Lillian, flouted the custom by volunteering her services as midwife and health practitioner to her neighbors. His father, Earl, carried on the more traditional role of the southern landowner, eventually expanding his holdings to 4,000 acres worked by mostly black tenant farmers. Earl Carter expanded his business dealings as peanut broker, warehouseman and retailer of farm supplies and equipment.

As president, Carter oversaw a reorganization of several executive branch departments to reflect his domestic priorities. The existing Department of Health, Education and Welfare was divided into two cabinet-level entities, the Department of Education and the Department of Health and Human Services. A new, cabinet-level Department of Energy was created. Throughout his term, President Carter sought to coordinate a national policy of energy conservation to reduce America's reliance on imported oil. At the same time, he pursued deregulation of transportation, communications, and finance.

Many of the Carter administration's most noteworthy accomplishments came in the field of foreign affairs. President Carter established diplomatic relations with the People's Republic of China and made good on a long-standing American promise to return control of the Panama Canal to the Panamanians. After negotiating the necessary treaties with Panama, Carter prevailed in an exceptionally contentious ratification fight in the Senate.

The outstanding achievement of the Carter presidency was the peace settlement between Israel and Egypt. Over 13 days of meetings at the presidential retreat, Camp David, Carter persuaded President Anwar Sadat of Egypt and Prime Minister Menachem Begin of Israel to end the 31-year state of war between their countries. Egypt was the first of Israel's Arab neighbors to make peace with the Jewish state. Israel ended its occupation of the Sinai peninsula and returned control of the territory to Egypt. President Carter later published his reflections on the Middle East conflict in his 1985 book, <u>The Blood of Abraham</u>.

President Carter also negotiated a Strategic Arms Limitation Treaty

(SALT II) with the Soviet Union, but before the Senate could vote to ratify the treaty, the Soviet Union invaded Afghanistan and Carter withdrew the treaty from consideration. The two superpowers agreed informally to abide by the terms of the treaty, even though neither side ever ratified it officially.

The 1979 revolution in Iran provided the most trying foreign policy challenges of the Carter presidency. After the victory of a fundamentalist Islamic faction in the Iranian revolution, radical students seized the American embassy and held American diplomatic personnel hostage, while demanding that the United States deliver the deposed Shah of Iran, who had sought medical care in the United States. Even after the Shah's departure from the United States and his subsequent death in Cairo, the government of Iran refused to return the American hostages. After an unsuccessful attempt to rescue the captive Americans, President Carter was able to secure the Iranian government's agreement to release the hostages, but not until after he had been defeated for re-election by Ronald Reagan.

Since leaving office, Jimmy Carter has been the most active of ex-Presidents. In 1982, he became University Distinguished Professor at Emory University, in Atlanta, Georgia, and in partnership with the University, founded the Carter Center to resolve conflict, promote democracy, protect human rights, and prevent disease around the world. Since 1989, observers from the Carter Center have monitored more than 60 elections in 25 countries.

President Carter has long served on the board of directors of Habitat for Humanity, a nonprofit organization that helps build homes for the needy in the United States and in other countries. He and Rosalynn Carter themselves volunteer with the organization for one week every year. Jimmy Carter also teaches Sunday school and is a deacon in the Maranatha Baptist Church of Plains.

Since leaving the White House, Jimmy Carter's personal diplomacy has helped to defuse international crises in hot spots from North Korea to Haiti. In 2002, he was awarded the Nobel Peace Prize for his efforts. With Theodore Roosevelt and Woodrow Wilson, he is the third American president to have been so honored. The Nobel committee cited former President Carter "for his decades of untiring effort to find peaceful solutions to international conflicts, to advance democracy and human rights, and to promote economic and social development."

Most ex-presidents publish a volume of memoirs or two, but Jimmy Carter has carried on an impressive career as an extremely prolific and successful author. As of this writing, he has published 20 books. In addition to his presidential memoir Keeping Faith, written shortly after he left office, he has written memoirs of childhood, books on religion, spirituality, aging and family life, a volume of verse, and a historical novel, The Hornet's Nest (2004), set in the South during the Revolutionary War. In his most recent work, Our Endangered Values: America's Moral Crisis (2005), he returns to the theme of morality in political leadership. From the day he entered public life, this has always been Jimmy Carter's first concern. It is that quality of moral leadership that has given him a unique role among all the men who have held the office of President of the United States.

Jimmy Carter and Friendship Force International

The Friendship Force was founded by Wayne Smith and introduced on March 1, 1977, by President Jimmy Carter at a White House gathering of state governors. At that time, President Carter asked the governors to return to their states and identify a volunteer leader who would serve as State Director for the Friendship Force in their state. Rosalyn Carter served as Honorary Chairperson until 2002.

Introduced March 1, 1977 – In order to make ends meet Jimmy devised a plan to cut expenses in half by inviting other family members to come and live in his household. They were able to save by not having to bear the cost of accommodation. It was Jimmy Carter's idea that created the Friendship Force and he is the true founder of Friendship Force. He sought Wayne Smith's help to promote his idea with other members and that is how Friendship Force came to be.

Mr. Ryoichi Sasakawa

President of The Japan Shipbuilding Industry Foundation, played an important role in the organization's history. After being introduced to the Friendship Force, Mr. Sasakawa became convinced of the worthy goals of the program. Thanks to Mr. Sasakawa's financial gifts in the mid 1980s, The Friendship Force was able to grow into a global network of independent chapters, which are called Friendship Force clubs. The clubs are organized and led by volunteers in more than 350 communities on six continents.

In the mid 1980's –However Mr. Sasakawa's financial gift was soon used-up by poor handling and by personal gain. (living high on the hog) by the Wayne Smith family. The concept of Friendship Force was Jimmy and Rosalyn Carter's idea of saving money, not spending recklessly for personal satisfaction.

In 1985, the A.R.M.S. (American Russian Mutual Survival) program was implemented under the auspices of The Friendship Force. The endeavor encouraged the use of arms that embrace rather than arms that destroy. In May of that year a group of 10 Soviet citizens traveled to the U.S. to extend arms of friendship in Atlanta, Georgia; Raleigh, North Carolina; Richmond, Virginia and Washington D.C. This was followed by a series of exchanges between the USA and the USSR, with thousands of Americans and Soviets participating. The success of the ARMS program demonstrated that the Friendship Force can be a powerful force for good in the world.

As a result of its initiatives between the United States and the Soviet Union, the Friendship Force was nominated in 1992 for The Nobel Peace Prize.

In addition to its annual series of exchanges between established Friendship Force clubs, Friendship Force International (FFI) conducts a variety of specialized programs. These include the "discover" series designed to introduce Friendship Force members to new countries and cultures, humanitarian and educational exchanges, and Friendship Festivals that include participants from many countries.

Since its founding in 1977, The Friendship Force has brought together millions of people. Today we are active in more than 50 countries, promoting friendship and goodwill through an extensive program of home hosting, or exchanges. In 2007 alone, 5763 friendship ambassadors traveled between 58 countries, with thousands more serving as hosts.

Friendship Force has clubs throughout many parts of the world.

Australia – Austria – Belarus – Belgium- Belize – Brazil – Bulgaria – Canada – Chili – China P. R.C – Colombia – Costa Rica – Cyprus – Czech Republic – Denmark – Egypt – Estonia – France – Georgia – Germany – Ghana – Hungary – India – Indonesia – Ireland – Israel – Italy – Japan – Jordan – Kenya – Kirghizstan – Korea- Latvia – Lithuania – Mexico – Moldavia- Netherlands – New Zealand- Norway – Peru – Philippines - Poland – Russia – Singapore - Slovakia – South Africa – Sweden- Taiwan R. O.C. – Thailand – Turkey – Ukraine – United Kingdom – United States – Uzbekistan - Vietnam

Friendship Force International is supported by membership, exchange fees, donations, and foundation grants.

Marshal McLuhan

The most important thinker since Newton, Darwin, Freud, Einstein and Pavlov; a very creative man who hit very large nails not quite on the head; McLuhan was a Canadian, a Professor of Literature and a convert to Catholicism (it gives him emotional stability), father of six children, four daughters and two sons. Born in Edmonton in 1911, he studied engineering and then literature at the University of Manitoba, Canada.

At Cambridge, England he pursued a study of literary influences which in time led him to develop a concern with communication of thought, emotion, and belief and with the consequences of transmission. He formed an early and continuing admiration for the techniques and artistic intentions of James Joyce, Ezra Pound and T.S. Eliot. He taught at the University of Wisconsin, St Louis University and University of Windsor. He served as Professor of Literature at the University of Toronto. He has published hundreds of articles and written four books, The Mechanical Bride and Folklore of Industrial Man (1951); The Gutenberg Galaxy: The Making of Typographic Man (1962); Understanding Media: The Extension of Man (1964); and The Medium is the Message: An Inventory of Effects (1967). His interest and direction forced him to reflect on every aspect of human existence, sensory, psychic and material. The Gutenberg Galaxy was awarded the Governor General's Award equivalent of the Pulitzer Prize in 1962. McLuhan's reputation was that of a nuisance and agitated protagonist shaped by English paternalism and American indifference.

It was the publication of Understanding Media in 1964 that gave McLuhan an extensive audience. It has inspired a torrent of criticism as well as almost euphoric discovery. Professor McLuhan explains that the term 'medium' is an extension of man whether it be a book, an automobile, an electric light bulb, television or clothes. His theory is that the media a man uses to extend his senses and his faculties will determine what he is, rather than the other way around.

There are historically ear oriented societies versus eye oriented and there is a great difference. It is only recently that literature has become the general environment for even a small part of the world. The differences between literate and pre-literate societies are enormous-examples are technological, mass production of identical items, after a millennia of making one object at a time and each somehow different from the other. The medium of print has influenced every facet of a literate society such as ours.

Teenagers are a distinctive group – McLuhan's theory is that this is the first generation of the electronic age. The medium that controls their environment is not print, it is television. The basic message of television is television itself, the process, just as the basic message of a book is print. As McLuhan says, "the Medium is the message." The new technologies, such as television, have become a new environment. They radically alter the entire way people use their five senses, the way they react to things, and therefore, their entire lives and the entire society are altered. The content doesn't matter.

The most profound effect of television-its real 'message' in McLuhan's terms- is the way it alters man's sensory patterns. The medium is the message is best known for McLuhanism Television-steps up the auditory sense and the sense of touch and depresses the visual sense-a paradox. A whole generation in America has grown up in the TV environment having the same kind of sensory reactions as African tribesmen. The same thing is happening all over the world. The world is growing into a huge tribe, a global village, in a seamless web of electronics. Today's new technologies-television, radio, the telephone, the computer-are causing another revolution. Print caused an 'explosion' – breaking society up into categories. The electronic media, on the other hand, are causing an 'implosion', forcing people back together in a tribal unity.

The sense is becoming dominant again primarily from radio, the telephone and the TV set.

The aural man is not so much of an individualist; he is part of a collective consciousness: he believes. The tribal man-the new TV generation is more apt at pattern recognition, which is the basis of computers. The child will learn a foreign language faster than a literate adult because he absorbs the whole pattern of the language, the intonations and the rhythms, as well as the meaning. The literate man is slowed down by the way he tries to convert the sounds to print in his mind and takes words one by one, categorizing them and translating them in plodding sequence.

As McLuhan sees it, there will be a great drop out from schools because TV-tribal children are aural people, tactile people, used to learning by pattern recognition. Today's classrooms are visual, literate, print minded by teachers. In the same way like these cities the print minded rulers keep on piling up around them more skyscrapers, more freeways pouring into them, more people piling into them. To the new drop out generation and the drop out generation to come, this idea of lateral space doesn't seem important.

Even visual people have begun to lose a little of the old idea of space because of the airplane. All anybody cares about is the time. For that matter-McLuhan says the drop out generation will even get rid of cars. The car is still largely tied to the idea of space, but the TV-tribal kids are not. It even shows up in their dances as when they stay in one place and create their own space, jerk around with the sound turned up; aural-tribal up into hot jolly hyper aesthetic decibels.

Eventually, says McLuhan, they will use the same kind of pattern in the way they work. They will work at home connected to the corporation, the boss, not by roads or railways but by television. They will relay information by closed-circuit two-way TV and by computer systems. The great massive American rush hour flow over all that asphalt surface, going to and from work every day, will be over. The only cars left will be sports cars; play things just like horses are today, a sport. Whole cities, especially New York, will end up just like cars, no longer vital to the nation but just play things.

More than anyone else, McLuhan realizes that there is so much that hasn't even been explored. He just keeps probing; he spins off theories like a Prophet. Many McLuhanites speak of him as a Prophet. It is only partly his visions of a future. It is more his extraordinary attitude, his demeanor, his qualities of monomania, of mission. He is not competing for status, his is alone on a vast unseen terrain, the walker through walls, the x-ray eye, an incredibly mysterious visionary of unfathomable depth beyond the comprehension of the majority of today's society.

Maurice Strong

Born in rural Manitoba, Canada, Maurice Strong is a visionary of renowned international stature. His superior ability to see the future in great depth and his action in bringing about changes which would not happen but for his genius has endowed him with a reputation of great respect and admiration as well as much sought after advice. See the internet for more information on his background.

Maurice Strong argues that the western media is wrong about China. Read: Marshal McLuhan's The Gutenberg Galaxy, The Limits of Power by Andrew J Bacevich at Boston University, "The Right is Wrong and the Left is Right" by Ed Finn as evidence, based on rational thinking.

In the August 18th 2008 edition of "Maclean's" magazine, Maurice Strong explains that as one who has been coming to China for more than 40 years he now spends most of his time there. He cannot help but contrast, with dismay what he sees and experiences there with the negative image to which so many in the west are exposed. Even after the tragic earthquake western media attempted to blame China for not acting more quickly, yet no government could have responded so efficiently and expeditiously to a disaster of such immense proportions, and few if any are better prepared to do so.

China has been making progress in building a vibrant, modern society, but inevitably it still has to cope with massive problems left by its turbulent past. China has raised more people out of poverty than any nation has ever done, and it is deeply committed to its objective of ensuring that those who have been left behind are able to participate in the benefits of its dynamic economy.

Advancements continue to be made in the movement toward more democratic processes and respect for human rights. The standards we exhort China to adopt are those we have only recently, and not yet fully, lived up to ourselves.

China is embarking on a distinctive and unprecedented pathway to a new model of development based on utilizing the methods of capitalism to achieve the goals of socialism-a socialist market economy. The entire world has a great stake in the success of China in making this transformation.

We should continue to facilitate China's full participation in the policy and decision making processes by which the future of all of us is being shaped. Climate change is an issue that is especially relevant. China realizes that it will be one of the most vulnerable victims of climate change and is already taking serious measures domestically to avert these risks. But it cannot be expected to transform these into binding commitments that are not matched by firm and enforceable commitments by the countries, notably the United States, whose accumulated emissions of greenhouse gases have caused the irreversible damage already inflicted on the world.

China's participation in the post-Kyoto agreements now being negotiated is necessary and will be forthcoming only on the basis of a fair sharing of responsibilities and obligation in which those who have contributed most to the problem of climate change must take the lead.

Similarly the attempt to shift the onus for increases in food, oil and commodity prices to China, as well as India and others now competing for these imports, will be counterproductive. The needs of the poor and the newly developing countries cannot be subordinated to the wasteful and indulgent appetites of the rich and their pre-emption of a disproportion of the world's resources.

But China will not and cannot be expected to be subservient to the decisions and influences of the small number of more developed nations that continue to assert dominance in international policy, decision making and institutions, which they have enjoyed for so long.

Uninformed and ideologically biased critics of China should ask themselves why it is that the majority of Chinese today are better off and better satisfied than ever.

The re-emergence of China as a world leader is one of the most important events of this period of history, and one that will have a profound and decisive impact on the future of the entire human community. This is the China we know and want the entire world to know. The Beijing Olympics, which focused the world spotlight on the new China, provided a unique opportunity for the world to view China as its people and friends do.

China will continue to defend its own frontiers and territories while respecting the sovereignty of its neighbors and resolving differences with them peacefully.

The alternative, in all these issues and others, is an ominous and growing potential for conflict at a time when what the world needs is a new and immensely increased degree of cooperation.

This requires a radical strengthening of the international agreement and institutions to foster extensive cooperation, particularly a revitalized United Nations and its agencies.

Canada will join hands with the one of the founders of Medicare, J.S. Wordsworth, and Municipal doctors, Dr Norman Bethume and Tommy Douglas, the latter two who are most beloved in China and in Canada. Canadians revere in each of their statures for bringing better health to the people in China and to the people in Canada. Each worked very hard in spite of many difficulties and opposition. They devoted their whole lives so that people in China and people in Canada could enjoy better health. They showed the world the way to better health and living by their own example. They were Visionaries - Heroes of Medicare in Canada and in China!

CHAPTER III:
RACISM IN CANADA AND THE UNITED STATES

The election of Barak Obama as a U.S. President does not prove that United States citizens are no longer racists. It does prove that many people voted for Obama because they saw him as their only hope to save them from poverty, loss of their jobs and loss of their homes, not because of anti-racism. Without any or enough income, they are not able to make mortgage payments. As a result mortgage companies are foreclosing on them. This is the same method mortgage companies used on farmers in Canada in the "Crash of 1929". People lost their farms. Jobs were scarce. When thousands of people demonstrated in Winnipeg, they were shot at. A man was killed as a result. He was the establishment's example of what awaited those who tried to protest.

The same people who voted for Obama also voted for George W. Bush. **They acted according to their best interest.** Racism is alive and well, in the U.S. and in, Canada.

During the Republican administration, Paul Robeson a celebrated singer was denied equal rights with whites and as a result he fled from the U.S. and immigrated to Russia. He was banned from the

U.S. Now, under President Obama, he will be allowed to return but it is a small victory, for the U.S. remains racist.

The American people were duped into believing that patriotism was reason enough to spend $648 billion to date because of former President George W. Bush's statement that "you are either with me or against me" not "that you have a right to your own opinion." George W. Bush was so successful in duping the American people that other countries saw this as an opportunity to invest in his successful scheme. In doing so, they have also put their economies at risk of complete collapse and of hardship for their people and their countries. This greed for oil and power has had its economic influence felt by the rest of the world as well. So it seems like there is no end to it. How did this come about or happen? We have lived under complete dominance of greed and power for the past centuries that has led us to our present situation. Our only hope is to change by helping each other rather than destroying each other. George W. Bush would never have condoned his action if he had seen its consequences. He must be forgiven.

I make an urgent appeal to dedicated people, to step up and support this vision. Your assistance can be made by funding faculties of medicine throughout our country. This will help rebuild the reputation and respect of the United States. US citizens who travel will now have assurance that they will be respected and accepted. The past President must work hard to restore the damages (done by brainwashing) sustained by the Iraqi people and the American military all because of American government greed for oil and power at the expense of its reputation and the lives of millions of people. Americans must now pay the Iraqi people in order to restore the simple necessities of everyday living, like electricity, water, safe travel to work and so on so, that these people can go on with their lives normally. This action will promote worldwide respect for the American government. The whole world knows that Saddam Hussein was victim of a U.S. "Kangaroo Court" because of George W. Bush's greed for oil and power.

In the past centuries, we have been dominated by power and greed with devastating results of pollution of air, water and soil, global warming, world obesity epidemic and nuclear threat. This system of government has proved to be detrimental to all civilization including itself. **The past system has failed and our only salvation is to seek change before it is too late. We must help each other, not destroy or kill each other (that's a horrible way to live).** I feel that had he seen the consequences of his actions, neither George W. Bush nor any other human being would have done what he did. He must be forgiven for he knew not what he was doing.

Before forgiveness, an apology is in order- a must! At a time, when it was in past president George W. Bush's interest to get oil from Iraq he cooperated with Saddam Hussein. At the same time Dick Cheney cooperated with Saddam in order to get access to Afghanistan's poppy seed drug business so he could negotiate with them to ensure safe transportation of oil from Iraq.

In addition to the above, the US along with other countries, participated in the division of Africa following World War 1 (Margaret Macmillan "Paris 1919- Six Months That Changed The World"). Africa was weak financially and vulnerable. African groups were competing for power amongst each other. They saw foreign help as a temporary solution to their problems but the foreigners stayed to fulfill their own interests. For the US, it was to get Iraqi oil and Afghanistan's drug business.

Following many years of foreign occupation (by colonial rule), Africans were very vulnerable and capitulated to further abuse by the US's pretence of helping. In fact the opposite is true, that the US helped themselves.

His search for weapons of mass destruction, an excuse President George Bush used to dupe his fellow Americans and other people in the world into believing that gave him the right to declare war on Iraq. He also thought that it gave him the right to hang Saddam Hussein.

How would you George W. Bush like to be hung at the pleasure of real Iraqi people (unlike your US dominated "Kangaroo" court?)

Remember the old saying "What's good for Goose is good for the Gander?" Do you believe it? Or is just good for the goose and, in your case, not the gander? Whose interests are you protecting and why? For greed of oil? Is that why you had Saddam Hussein hung? Is that why thousands and thousands of people were duped into thinking that in giving up their lives, they were helping their country and conforming to your idea of "patriotism"?

Your economy is based on war. Manufactured materials are used in wars. Reckless and corrupt, an invoice for an ordinary hammer was listed at a cost of $500.00! at US tax payer's expense. Former President Dwight Eisenhower warned the US government that depending on an economy based on military use would hurt US image and Americans would be disliked. This is exactly what happened causing many US tourists to pose as Canadian citizens for their safety and security.

Your ease in brainwashing the US citizens, and because of other countries' greed in which they copied similar investments (like the Australians) resulted in the same economic disaster as has now destroyed the US economy leaving its people in desperate situations with loss of jobs and unable to make payments. This huge war debt has had a "domino" effect on all countries in the world today. To think of it all happening as a result of your greed! Some governments have fallen and others still will fall. Iceland suffered deeply under the global financial meltdown that led three major banks in the country to fold last fall. Iceland's government recently collapsed. The Prime minister of Iceland has demanded the resignation of the country's three governors, of the central bank.

In Iceland angry citizens were demonstrating, looting and attempting to leave their country and their culture in order to make a living and get a new start. Some were coming to Gimli, in Winnipeg in Manitoba Canada where there is an Icelandic community.

I am putting this in plain and simple language versus politically correct. You are worse than an ordinary thief. You lied, you cheated, you deceived and you murdered. You and Dick Cheney, Rush Limbaugh and other so called "Hawks" all destroyed the US economy and the world's view of the US. You must all admit your crimes and all apologize for your greed and for your true intentions if you wish to be forgiven.

Many people have died because of your anti stem cell treatment ideology. Would you refuse stem cell treatment if your life depended on it? After hiding his affliction with Parkinson's disease for a number of years Michael J Fox came out and revealed that he has Parkinson's disease. He wanted to help others by having them watch for signs of Parkinson's and to tell them how to help live with it. You President George Bush refused his plea. To refuse to help a man whose only wish was to help others is cruel beyond belief! What do you say in your defense?

Millions of people have died and suffered as a result of your actions based on greed. Your "hawks" also contributed in no small way to destroying the US economy and the US world image. Russ Limbaugh's "Holier –than-thou" attitude toward former president Clinton was a futile attempt to discredit him. President Clinton worked very hard for his country. He is a great credit to the US but you Russ Limbaugh contributed nothing but constant and relentless criticism. What kind of contribution is that? And for whose sake?

I think it is high time for you all to take a good look at yourselves and do the honorable thing. Beg for forgiveness, before you are extradited by American people who will decide whether they want to give up their lives to save you and your families. Are you willing to take this chance? I hope not for all your sakes.

There are extreme radical Muslims in Iraq, Iran and in the rest of the world who would not hesitate to issue an ultimatum to US citizens to extradite all members of the Bush, Cheney, Limbaugh families or risk a nuclear attack on the US. What do you think the people of the US would choose to do? To give up their lives for you? There isn't a soul on this earth who has not been affected both financially and socially by your Iraqi war debt. Why would anyone on this earth give up their life for you, because of your greed for power and control? Only one thing can save you from this disaster. You must publicly apologize to everyone in the world, since everyone has been affected in one way or another by your lies and your greed for oil and power. It's time to "Payback". (See Margaret Atwood) This is not unlike Nelson Mandela's forgiveness of apartheid in Africa.

Following this apology, you must all do penance by doing deeds that prove that you are truly repentant and wish to make amends. This will require hard work on your parts. Only then will the people of the world forgive you. It will take some time to accomplish this goal of forgiveness. Once hurt, people will not be easily fooled.

Age of philanthropy

Society can no longer depend on government to come to the rescue of its needs. This is an age of Philanthropy - an age of compassion, of helping the desperate needs of the hungry, the sick, the abandoned, and the orphaned children. It is a time of sharing and making a difference, giving hope and relief to millions of people. The wisest and most loving Sri Sri Ravi-Shankar says,

"Life is sacred. Celebrate life. Care for others and share whatever you have with those less fortunate than you. Broaden your vision, for the whole world belongs to you. This is Enlightenment - a state of being so mature and unshakable by any circumstance." (Gautier)

CHAPTER IV:
MEDICAL FACULTY SPONSORSHIP

Canadian superstar Celine Dion will lead Canadians in sponsoring a Faculty of Medicine of her choice. Because of her great love for her country, Canada, and her fierce love of her family, Celine Dion will be the first one to sponsor a Faculty of Medicine. All Canadians will appreciate Celine for leading the way of sponsorship.

Celine and her family will have the best healthcare possible. Celine will have the satisfaction and the guarantee of knowing that her immediate and extended family will be taken care of for the rest of their lives with the latest in medical research.

She will receive personal heartfelt satisfaction from students, graduates, specialists, etc. who will write personal letters of gratitude to her. They will be people who otherwise may never have been able to enter the profession of their choice because of financial circumstance or location etc.

Philanthropists who contribute or invest in a faculty of medicine of their choice will do so willingly and become active partners with the students and/or graduates of their sponsored medical faculty. Their investment and generosity will provide free tuition to students so that they are not faced with huge debts upon graduation but will be contributing by way of income tax, adding to the economy.

Canada is proud and grateful to other home-grown philanthropists such as J Brett Wilson, The Thomson Family, Ted Rogers Jr., Galen Weston, Paul Desmarais Sr, Irving Family, Jimmy Pattison, Jeff Skoll, Mike Lazaridis, Jim Balsille, Barry Sherman, Belinda Stronach, David Suzuki, Arthur Latcham, The Saputo family, Fred and Ron Mannix, Carlo Fidani, The Asper family, The Richardson family, Michael Degroote, Marcel Adams, Mitchell Goldhar, Albert Latner, Seymour Schulich, the Greenberg family, Peter Nygard, Stewart Blusson, Andre Chagnon, Peter Gilan, Randall Moffat, The Libfeld family, Jeff Skoll, Louise Blouin MacBain, Douglas Fregin, John P. Loewen, Martin Bergen, Miriam Bergen, and Marcel Desautels.

Canada acknowledges and is most grateful to U.S. philanthropists for their generosity and help by giving: such as Madonna, Donald K. Johnson, Richard Kroft, Elizabeth Taylor, Tiger Woods and Drew Barrymore.

International Philanthropists: Princess Diana, whose dedication and successful achievement in helping others is admired by the whole world. Her untimely death came as such a great shock, that she is mourned to this day. The hopes and dreams of Canadians today are for her sons, William and Harry, to continue Dianna's mission of philanthropy.

In North America, Canadians are blessed with renowned people like John Paulson, Louie Navellier and Associates, Warren Buffett, Bill and Linda Gates, Oprah Winfrey, Rosalynn and Jimmy Carter (founders of Friendship Force International).

In Britain, the Royal Family, Sir Richard Branson.

In Africa, Bono, Bob Geldolf, Angelique Kiljo, And Yannick Noah. Examples of supreme giving of themselves, from Africa and India are Nelson Mandela, Rev. Desmond Tutu, Mother Theresa, Mahatma Gandhi, and Dr. Martin Luther King of North America.

Examples of Home-grown giving of themselves from Canada are W. Brett Wilson and Stephen Lewis, who has worked tirelessly to save children in Africa from AIDS, and Dr. Victor G. Millan, M.Sc. (MB) whose work in angioplasty laid a foundation for others to continue his life-saving work and John Ralston Saul who has worked tirelessly in all parts of Canada, particularly in the north. In terms of our sovereignty he helped us to recognize this our land is native, always was, is, and shall always continue to be. There is no need to spend huge sums of money to establish something that already exists. It is better to use the money to invest in individuals' education and career. Having been left behind and ignored for so long, it's time to catch up and be themselves.

There are those philanthropists whom Canadians are not that familiar with, but to whom Canadians are grateful wherever you may be. Your generosity in giving to those in need is an everlasting act making this a better world for all its inhabitants.

By participating in the Art of Living program, Canada, China and India have a better chance to succeed in establishing many more Art of Living locations when these countries are financially, psychologically and spiritually comfortable and when they have Universal Health Care and Early Childhood Care and Free Education. It may take ten to twenty years for this to happen.

Learning to help each other will pass on from one generation to another – first in the family, then in the community and eventually the world. The ideas expressed in this book may appear too idealistic to some people but nothing ventured, nothing gained.

If only to make a small dent by opening some people's eyes and/or their minds to the fact that there is another way to make changes will be well worth writing this book.

Ed Finn, Editor of Canadian Center for Policy Alternatives (CCPA) points out that CCPA, although not an activist organization itself does the research that underpins many of the campaigns against corporate wrong doing. And he expresses this hope in his essays: "Perhaps a few of my ideas may even inspire some activists or provide them with ammunition in their front-line skirmishes". As many activists will affirm, Ed Finn's ideas have done just that in the past, still do, and will continue to inform and inspire others in the ongoing struggle for a better world. He would be the last one to take any credit for the mounting opposition to excessive business influence in Canada and around the world, but he was certainly one of the first writers and editors to challenge corporate power and expose its ruinous effects.

TENURE

Strong government leaders are needed in order to succeed with these plans.

Prime Minister Stephen Harper has been re-elected and is the best and most suitable choice for leading Canada to become the most prosperous country in the world. Harper supporters are very dedicated to him. Prime Minister Harper, Leader of the Conservative Party of Canada, is both visionary and determined. He has great confidence and a quiet analytical mind, quick to take strategic advantage of any given situation. Canadians need his expertise and dedication.

President Obama will have an onerous task. He must first try and restore dignity and badly needed respect for the U.S. He must beg forgiveness for all the people who died at home and abroad as a result of greed for oil. He must remain humble and help restore damages in those countries ravaged by war, so those remaining people can go on with their daily tasks. They need electricity, water, food and safety measures of health etc. Only in this way will the U.S regain the badly needed respect and confidence of people abroad – **not by force of power or weaponry but by peaceful and helpful ways.** But all this comes at a great cost. If the U.S can raise billions of dollars for war, then why not for peace? There is plenty of money in the world owned by very few people. Some of that money has been given freely to help others who are less fortunate and in grave need. Millions of children are starving, homeless and orphaned. Here is an opportunity for those few very rich to continue to help others. Amongst them are such renowned people as Warren Buffett, Bill Gates, Oprah Winfrey, and Sir Richard Branson. Canada is beholden to them for their contribution and wishes to <u>specially</u> acknowledge them for showing the world how and what it means to help those in need.

PHILANTHROPIC SPONSOR BENEFITS

- A written acknowledgement from each medical student for their sponsor's generosity and what it has meant to them personally
- Regular reports to sponsor from medical students on their progress while in training
- Assurance that the sponsor will receive the best healthcare at all times, coordinated by the Dean of the Faculty
- Satisfaction in knowing you will be taken care of by a large number of caring and appreciative medical practitioners, specialists, nurses etc. At no time will you be alone. One person will always be there to safeguard any change in your health status.
- An opportunity of assurance and access to the utmost in healthcare at the same time of giving back to society and benefiting everyone.
- Achieve satisfaction by leaving a legacy of good works

through the investment in people's overall health and well being and help those who would otherwise not become doctors, nurses and researchers.

In giving you get. Canadian society appreciates and is grateful for the heartfelt contributions of philanthropists worldwide. You have made a tremendous difference, saving lives, giving hope and showing you care. God knows the world needs you.

People will be able to see themselves as part of a human race, the same species, helping each other, developing their own personal skills in art, music, writing etc. They will be rid of stress to compete so they will be happier, more energized and more able to take on their world in peace and harmony.

CHAPTER V:
UNIVERSITY OF SASKATCHEWAN

Message from Dean Graham Scoles "In with the New"

When a change in the name of the College was first suggested and since June 2006 when that change was approved, we have had considerable discussion with our stakeholders and alumni about our vision for the future. Some voice concern that in redefining ourselves, we might lose sight of our traditional roots, but with continued discussion and with words such as bio-economy and bio-products becoming more widely used and understood (not to mention high oil prices), it has become easier to explain the reason for change.

Those discussions have proven invaluable, not only because they've brought our community into a lively discourse about the College's future but because they've brought even greater clarity to our refreshed mandate. To clarify: our new mission is that through our teaching and research we will advance the responsible use of land, water and biological resources to provide products and services that enhance the quality of life. This mandate is based on the fact that we must increasingly depend on the world's biological resources to provide our needs. In one sense, this mission takes us back to before the industrial revolution; in another, it is a compelling vision of a sustainable future and represents a significant opportunity for our students and our province.

In whatever way we choose to plot our path forward, rest assured we would continue to draw upon our recognized history in agricultural research. The body of knowledge residing in our College comprises the very roots of our authority, providing us with the opportunity to take a leadership role in the emerging bio-economy. And although we cannot see the precise outlines of our future, we are more confident than ever that with this strong foundation beneath us, the College of Agriculture and Bio-resources will continue as an international leader in applied research and scholarship.

You'll read more in the pages to follow of our new initiatives and the progress we've made over the past year. We now have students in the second year of a new degree for the College - the Bachelor of Science in Agribusiness. Another degree program, the Bachelor of Science in Renewable Resource Management was approved at University Council in November. After so many years as a college offering a single degree, this change in our programming has forced us to stretch our imaginations and our resources. The results have been welcomed as they've brought us new faculty and students whose enthusiasm for our direction is contagious.

Another significant step forward this past year was the development of two proposals that form part of our 2008 to 2012 Integrated Plan submission. Building on the Certificate in Indigenous Peoples Resource Management Program (funded by Indian and Northern Affairs Canada), we have proposed the establishment of an Indigenous Land Management Institute (ILMI). This Institute will perform research and train graduate students, and also help us to offer undergraduate training beyond the certificate level through a diploma and eventually a degree program.

Also in 2007, we stated our intention to establish ourselves as a major bio-economy center for North American. It is clear to us that because we already have so much of the talent and resources necessary to facilitate a center of this kind, our college is the obvious choice for such an initiative. We are fortunate too in that our discussions with the Province of Saskatchewan on this and other proposed programs have been so fruitful: the government has supported us generously with investments in our infrastructure and our people. I can tell you that this is a relationship other universities in Canada envy and admire.

You will note the theme of this issue of Acknowledge is 'international exchange', and that the stories herein take us from Saskatchewan to Mongolia, China, Peru, Ethiopia, Japan, Sweden, India, the US and back again. We have our faculty and students to thank for this creative trading of knowledge between universities and nations: it is mainly due to their initiative and energy that such fruitful interchange is possible.

BIO-BUSINESS, FIRST STEPS TO
A NEW KIND OF BOOM

Establishing the College of Agriculture and Bio-resources as a North American bio-economy center is a major focus for the college in coming years, say senior AgBio academics.

That goal is possible because 'we have literally everything in place at the University of Saskatchewan to make it so', says Agriculture and Bio-resources College Acting Dean Graham Scoles.

On the campus itself, we have the complete cluster of life sciences - everything from agriculture and biosciences, engineering and business to medicine, pharmacy and veterinary sciences.

In addition, we work with a significant group of industry players, either on this campus at Innovation Place or very close by. These organizations include Agriculture and Agrifood Canada and AgWest Bio, to name just a few.

Indeed, Scoles notes the Conference Board of Canada recently completed a major review of the entire bioresources industry and concluded that going forward, we are the obvious choice for a bio-economy center. Clearly, we have the people and the resources to make this compelling vision a reality.

With those assets firmly behind it, the College of Agriculture and Bioresources has joined forces with the Edwards School of Business and the College of Engineering to develop a bio-economy center at the U of S. Dr Bernard Laarveld, Professor with the University of Saskatchewan's College of Agriculture and Bioresources, is the lead for the project.

Knowing that the concept of bio-economy is an unfamiliar or obscure one for many laypeople, he describes it as 'a new industry that provides sustainable economic benefits by using renewable biomass production, processing and refining to produce bio-energy and bioproducts.

It is important to remember that these products include not only industrial but also health-related products and services. Close all oil refineries in Canada and in all foreign countries in exchange for their economic recovery.

Laarveld says the emergence of bio-economy as a new model is driven by a number of factors: first, growing public concern about the environment, climate change and public/private need for sustainable resource management: second, the recognition that fossil fuels are finite and their supply increasingly insecure: third, the accelerating growth of the world economy and its accompanying demand for energy, food and bioproducts.

"We also see major business and economic opportunities in the emerging bio-economy through the industry's introduction of 'green' products and services", he says." On top of that, we see the bio-economy providing diversification and rejuvenation of the rural economy in Saskatchewan."

He notes that one of the main challenges facing the proposed center is a need to emphasize commercialization and research aligned with industry need. "We'll do this by focusing on the demand-pull approach of commercialization of technology by establishing public/private partnerships at early stages of the innovation cycle."

"Continued industry and investor involvement throughout the innovation cycle ensures efficiency and effective commercialization. Once applied to the bio-economy, this 'demand pull' principal should ensure that technology transfers are more collaborative, creative and successful." He notes the public private partnering and demand pull commercialization will attract increased investment as the research preformed will be better targeted to the end user with much greater assurance of success, thus lowering investment risk. You can imagine how this intergrading of forces would considerably speed up progress in bio-economy technology."

Partnering with Bernard Laarveld in the proposed center is the university's new dean of engineering Dr Janucz Kozinski. He agrees Canada could benefit from a stronger link between business and academia.

"But if you are going to have collaboration, it has to be a meaningful and equal partnership," he urges. "Whatever else we do, our research community in Canada must become more business focused and really concentrate on commercialization."

Kozinski see obvious synergies between the traditionally warring faction of fossil fuel and bio-fuel producers;" for one because Canada's future energy portfolio must be balance and properly diversified. There is obviously a roll for petroleum in our future and there is likely a roll for nuclear energy here too, especially when you consider the fact that in Saskatchewan we have 70% of the world high-quality uranium reserves. And there is of course a place for biofuels and bio-energy."

Why this diversity and not simply a clean break into the bio-economy? "Because I think in the new term we have to put our major emphasis on efficiencies," says Laarveld.

"Ethanol won't simply replace gasoline - that will never happen. Our greatest challenge today is thinking more strategically and in terms of multi-faceted fuel supply. That is why it is important to develop partnerships with energy companies in Alberta, to gauge their level of interest and see how we might work together."

But there is one point that professor Laarveld is not willing to bend; "Saskatchewan was the first in Canada to bring in an ethanol mandate so we already have the research capacity and the history to take a confident lead in this new industry."

Dean Scoles agrees. "When you're talking about bio-economy you are thinking in terms of land and resources - and let's remember that Saskatchewan has approximately 45% of the arable land in Canada as well enormous forestry resources in the northern part of the province.

"We are also seeing significant interest in bio-economy in both the federal and provincial governments, whose collective aim is to stimulate activity in this area through networking and attracting private players to the industry."

"We have a strong vision and great opportunities ahead for our faculty and our students. It's a great time to be focusing on bio-economy."

BRIDGE TO CHINA, THE SLEEPING GIANT

Building On A Stronger Relationship

A long-standing relationship with China's agricultural universities has recently evolved into a significant opportunity for the College of Agriculture and Bioresources says its dean.

"We've trained many Chinese graduate students at the College over the years, but we are now beginning to define a plan to educate their senior under graduate students as well, "says Acting Dean Graham Scoles, also a molecular geneticist and plant sciences professor at the University.

"A second component in our plan is a potential change in faculty; they have people who want to study in Canada and, similarly, we have people who would be delighted to spend a short period of time at a Chinese university.

"I see the potential for collaborations between our universities as extremely productive and exciting."

Scoles explains that the usual route for Chinese graduate students to the University of Saskatchewan as for every grad student; is with an application and request for funding." Traditionally, grad students would be provided funding by stipends from professors or through university/college scholarships in order to be able to afford to be able to study in Canada."

He notes that while the Chinese standard of living is only about only a fifth of the Canadian norm, "especially when it comes to salaries," some of China's universities and the parents of some Chinese students now have sufficient funding to support their own best-and brightest graduate and under-graduate students in a foreign academic setting. When you have a population of 1.3 billion people your universities are able to draw from a large financial base. He notes, "China sees numerous challenges and opportunities for its people, and it's no longer shy about pursuing educational options for its talent."

But as noted, graduate students aren't the only ones considered for the exchange, says Scoles. "I've been talking to Chinese administrators who are interested in a 'two-plus-two' program for their senior agriculture undergraduates. These students would complete two years of undergraduate studies in China, and then transfer here for the remaining two.

"What's even better is that these young students are extremely motivated and keen, and their parents anxious to support them in every way - and that includes financial support."

Scoles says there are over 60 agricultural universities in China; in the past few months he's visited the China Agriculture University in Beijing ("the top agriculture school in the country"), Jilin Agriculture University on Changchun and Shenyang Agriculture University, and he has been in contact with others. He believes these contacts must be maintained on an annual basis to make the linkages work and expects faculty will want to create their own research collaborations with Chinese scholars.

"We now have a fairly well worn path between our two countries, and I find their people very open to new opportunities for cooperation.

"In fact, many of the senior people in these universities graduated from the University of Saskatchewan back in the 1960's and 1970's. It's wonderful to meet these folks as I tour their universities - they clearly look back at their time in Saskatoon with great fondness."

CHAPTER VI:
ABROAD IN INDIA AND CHINA

Canada recognizes and values the long standing relationship with China's agricultural universities with Acting Dean Graham Scoles, a Molecular Geneticist and Plant Sciences Professor at the University of Saskatchewan, in Saskatoon and his vision for the future growth of world economy. Professor Scoles and the Honorable Lloyd Axworthy, University of Winnipeg, will develop a program of medical personnel recruitment by establishing close relations with present Canadian universities increasing the number of graduates and by building Canadian sponsored universities in China and in India in order to get its medical graduates who will immigrate to Canada to fulfill Canadian Healthcare needs.

They will encourage additional implementation of English and/or French Immersion programs in China and India's public school system beginning in kindergarten. A foreign language is easier to learn when started at a very young age. The reason for the language program is to eventually provide a common bond of communication for medical graduate immigrants, thus developing a common ground enabling people to see each other as the same species, "Human Kind", rather than by skin color, size or shape. Friendships will develop through common interests. By providing free tuition many more people of China and India, from lower income or rural backgrounds, will have access and opportunity to pursue their chosen careers DEBT FREE.

Graduates from these Universities will help fulfill Canadian Medicare needs according to former President of the Canadian Doctors Association, Dr. Brian Day's analysis. Graduates will have certain obligations to fulfill upon immigrating to Canada regarding Tenure and Philanthropic Sponsorship. Those graduates who wish to immigrate elsewhere must pay back all fees at once or the foreign institution that hires them will pay their debt estimated at $158,728 to over $200,000.

Canada will promote Early Childhood Education where children in Canada will learn to speak English, French, Mandarin and Himdu and a native aboriginal language. Children in China will learn to speak English, French, Himdu and children in India will learn to speak English, French and Mandarin. Each country's children will be expected to retain their local dialect.

CHAPTER VII:
PHILOSOPHY, RELIGIONS AND GLOBAL WATCHDOGS

All three nations Canada, India & China will encourage the study of all religions. There are 10 Major Religions in the world. Six from the Far East and four from the Middle East. In the Far East Hinduism is the oldest. Then came Buddhism, Jainism, Taoism, Shintoism and Sikhism. From the Middle East, Zoroastrianism is the oldest and then came Judaism, Christianity and Islam. Three of the Middle Eastern religions are rooted in the Old Testament: Islam, Christianity and Judaism. In the Far East, Shintoism and Taoism have completely different sources. Buddhism, Jainism and Sikhism have roots in Hinduism.

Far Eastern religion with different backgrounds coexists peacefully.

Middle Eastern religions with common roots have conflicts.

Far East - Six religions have peacefully coexisted and intermingled over the centuries.

Buddhism and Taoism completely accepted each other.

Manitoba Interfaith Council and the University of Winnipeg

Rev. Fredrich Ulrich of the Manitoba Buddhist Temple

"I wonder how my colleagues would feel if we would start an interfaith community group and invite "atheists"? "Religion can be liberating and restricting at the same time, but mostly it should be a path to the divine. I have come to realize no human being can understand God. In our ignorance there is room for agnostics, atheists and a tired old Buddhist. We need to get beyond ourselves."

Sikh leader Hakam Singh Johal, "Everyone has the right to his own religion, his own way, as long as he is not forcing his religion on anyone else, just look at the good parts and ignore the bad parts. Our religion believes one flower is not as beautiful as a bouquet. We believe that when all human beings get together it is more beautiful than one person.

Rev. Larry Pinsker, "It seems to me that one of the tasks I need to pursue is at what point do I stop listening and agree to disagree? I would ask how much we are prepared to give up and live in peace with each other."

Rev. Robert Hankinson, "Interfaith (dialogue) is about sharing respect for one's self, one's tradition, and the traditions of one's . I think we have grown in the understanding that we are one faith among many."

GLOBAL WATCHDOGS

A global Watchdog has identified what is said were the world's most corrupt foreign heads of government, singling out leaders of Indonesia, The Philippines, and the former Zaire.

The abuse of political power for private gain deprives the most needy of vital public services, creating a level of despair that breeds conflict and violence. It also hits the pockets of taxpayers and shareholders worldwide.

Determined to show the high cost of political embezzlement, Transparency International said that Suharto, Indonesia's president from 1967 to 1998, embezzled between $15 billion and $35 billion from a nation where the per capita gross domestic product is $695.

Former Philippines leader, Ferdinand Marcos, was second on the list, the group said, for taking between $5 billion and $10 billion.

Third was Mobutu Sese Seko, leader of Zaire, the African nation now known as Congo. Transparency International said he embezzled $5 billion.

Disgraced former Philippine president Joseph Estrada denied he had plundered $77 million from the country.

Other former leaders in the top ten were: Sani Abacha of Nigeria; Serbian leader Slobodan Milosevic; Jean Claude Duvalier of Haiti; Alberto Fujimori of Peru; Pablo Lazarenko of Ukraine; and Arnaldo Aleman of Nicaragua.

WORLD SAFETY

World Won't Be Safer After War in Iraq writes C. Don Palmer. "The Bush administration has accused Iraq of falsifying the account of its weapons program. The question we should ask ourselves is, does the U.S. have a monopoly on the truth? Through shameless manipulation, coercion and intimidation it was able to get the United Nations Security Council resolution for military action against Iraq if it harbors weapons of mass destruction. It is now evident that the weapons sleuths dispatched to Baghdad are on a fishing expedition. Even though they are making up the rules as they go along, they are unable to uncover any such weapons and have resorted to harassing the Iraqi people. This is pathetic. For the United States to claim that it wants to question Iraqi scientists about Iraq's weapons program on neutral ground is comical. What it wants is to massage, cajole, and stage the evidence it wants from such people.

The United Sates has designed its enemies based on its own dictates and it is prepared to act where or when it chooses. It has declared the United Nations irrelevant if it does not abide by its wishes. If the issue is about weapons of mass destruction, why isn't the President waiting for the weapons inspectors' report before war-mongering? It seems Bush has his own agenda and has shrouded his perfidy and duplicity in the United Nations Security Council resolution. It is indeed tragic to see a democratic nation so lacking in moral fiber. Given such arrogance and self-centerd behavior by the U.S., it is doubtful it will ever be respected for its principles, only feared for its weapons of mass destruction. **Military action against Iraq will do nothing to make the U.S. secure against terrorism, and the President is deluding himself if he thinks otherwise."**

CHAPTER VIII:
RECOMMENDATIONS TO THE PRIME MINISTER OF CANADA

Prime Minister Harper has been re-elected to a minority government, but that will quickly change to a majority by the following strategies:

- Bring Canadian Troops Back Home from Afghanistan Immediately
- Implement Kyoto Protocol Re: Global Warming
- Save the Canadian Health Care Plan and Money
- Ban all Nuclear Weapons
- Suspend Tar Sands Operations

VIII.1 - Bring Canadian Troops Back Home from Afghanistan Immediately

This issue was the top priority of the Liberal, N.D.P., and the Green Parties in their campaigns. Prime Minister Harper automatically gets their votes, which gives him a majority government. His opponents will appreciate his action. Prime Minister Harper will gain greater respect and admiration by the majority of Canadians and the world for his strategic decision.

Gilles Duceppe, Leader of the opposing Bloc Quebecois Party

did not support this issue because Quebec produces uranium used in producing nuclear weapons. Quebec is the world's largest producer of uranium. Quebec irresponsibly exports uranium to countries without regard for its use or consequence. Canada now ranks sixth among NATO countries in total military spending, and is the sixth-largest supplier of military goods to the world.

VIII.2 - Implement Kyoto Protocol Re: Global Warming

"Canada has become a world leader in sabotaging the UN's Rotterdam Convention, which is designed to protect life and the environment from hazardous chemicals such as asbestos".

Two years ago, the Chemical Review Committee recommended that chrysotile asbestos be listed as a product that required prior informed **consent** before being exported. The recommendation was approved by over 100 UN member countries, but Canada, together with India, Ukraine, Kyrgyzstan, Iran and Peru, flatly refused to let the Convention's process work and blocked action on the recommendation. They were joined by Russia, Indonesia and Zimbabwe, which have not ratified the Convention.

Canada's excuse for blocking the recommendation to restrict the export of asbestos was that no action should be taken to implement the Convention unless every single country agrees.

'This is a death sentence for the Convention,' said Joan Kuyek of Mining Watch Canada."

Prime Minister Harper will implement Canadian Kyoto Protocol targets to reduce greenhouse gases (carbon emissions). It may even be too late.

Kobe, Japan – The world is losing momentum in the battle against global warming, the United Nations climate chief warned, urging environmental ministers from wealthy countries to revive the effort by setting clear targets for reducing greenhouse gases.

The ministers gathered in the western Japanese city of Kobe for a three-day meeting as evidence mounted that rising world temperatures have been taking a toll on the planet at a faster rate than previously forecast.

The officials from the group of 8 countries, joined by representatives from other countries including China and other organizations, were to lay the foundations for the upcoming G8 summit in northern Japan in July '08.

Prime Minister Harper will join forces with world famous conservationists Dr. David Suzuki and former Vice-President of the United States, Al Gore thus gaining world attention and admiration for his strategic move. Canadians will be overwhelmed with pride. Again Prime Minister Harper will increase his majority and expand his popularity worldwide. Prime Minister Harper will now be the most respected and most enviable leader of any country in the world.

The opposing Bloc Quebecois Party claims that there is no proof that global warming is a recent occurrence rather than a natural occurrence. Many studies prove otherwise.

The recent cyclone hit in Irrawaddy Delta in Yangon, Myanmar and in Oklahoma City. – "A slow moving storm packing tornadoes and hail slammed rural Oklahoma destroying several buildings, tearing up trees, and tossing a mobile home onto a highway. The bodies of two storm victims were found in Kansas. No injuries were reported in Oklahoma. The pace of the storm was slow for a system producing so many tornadoes, said Daryl Williams, a meteorologist with the National Weather Service office."

Yangon, Myanmar – Aid agencies prepared to go into Myanmar's cyclone-hit Irrawaddy Delta after the country's ruling junta vowed to open its doors to help on the eve of an international donors meeting.

After weeks of stubbornly refusing assistance, Myanmar's ruling generals have told the United Nations that they are now willing to allow workers of all nationalities to go into the devastated Delta to assess the damage.

The ability to make such assessments will be the essential element in aid pledges from foreign governments.

An estimate released by the United Nations said that of the total 2.4 million people affected by the storm, about 42 percent had received some kind of emergency assistance."

People are still recovering from Hurricane Katrina (August 29, 2005) that hit New Orleans in Louisiana wiping a whole city away. People everywhere are subject to these and various other types of disasters by nature's design. Have people caused these disasters by altering the ozone layer with pollution or are they natural occurrences? One way or another they are disastrous in terms of loss of lives and of great financial burden.

Prime Minister Harper will implement a program by using a Richter-Scale measure so that people can be evacuated beforehand and not after a storm occurs. The world will look at Canada's Prime Minister as a savior and one who will solve their problems. Earthquakes can be detected prior to the occurrence by using the Richter Scale, thus saving many lives, factories, houses, rice fields, fruit trees, etc. The destruction caused by the earthquakes in Myanmar, and in Chengd, China, is estimated at $11 billion U.S.

Bogota, Columbia – A moderate earthquake shook the Columbian capital killing at least six people and injuring more than ten. The preliminary 5.6 magnitude quake shook buildings and sent residents running into the streets. Columbian Interior Minister

Carlos Holguin confirmed six people were killed by falling rocks and earth on a highway between Bogota and Villavicencio. The earthquake started around 2:20 p.m. and was centered about 50 kilometers southeast of the capital, the U.S. Geological Survey said.

VIII.3 - Save the Canadian Health Care Plan and Money

Canadians will save Canadian Medicare and Money by addressing all areas of need according to Former President of Canadian Doctors Association, Dr. Brian Day's recommendations. Nothing is more precious to Canadians than their Universal Healthcare Plan. It is the envy of most of the world. Canadian heroes, first and foremost, are the Aboriginals of Healthcare. They saved foreigners from starvation and disease because of their knowledge of medicine. Almost all of our medicine today has its origins in medicinal Herbs used by Aboriginals. Original discovery of medicine and its practice was by the Aboriginal people of North America.

Other heroes of Canadian Healthcare are, first and foremost, J.S. Wordsworth, who had both a strong faith and deep commitment to social justice. He had a desire to incorporate the positive values of forgiveness, dignity and acceptance of the poor and marginalized. Municipal Doctors, Tommy Douglas and Dr. Norman Bethume, (who volunteered his lifetime by helping sick people in China {like Doctors without Borders today}). Now the Canadian Healthcare Plan is in grave jeopardy because of the **cost** and **lack of medical personnel**. There will be changes and reforms so that the medical profession isn't such a time consuming profession - drawing the line on overtime hours and more focused on lifestyle.

Canada needs a huge increase in population in order to develop a strong and viable economy – one that would greatly increase income tax revenue. In exchange for Health Care Graduates (immigrants), China and India would receive, (as much as is available) food (grains, canola, and fish) oil, clean water, technology in: soil erosion, multiple crop production, and pollution control allowing for a cleaner environment. Canada will help China and India design a universal Health Care Program to relieve stress and create healthier and happier nations.

PRESIDENT OF CANADIAN MEDICAL ASSOCIATION - SAVING CANADIAN MEDICARE AND MONEY

Canada will save Medicare and Money by addressing all areas of need according to one of the former Presidents, Dr. Brian Day's recommendations. Nothing is more precious to Canadians than their Universal Medicare. **Medicare is in jeopardy because of the cost and lack of medical personnel.**

Dr. Day has identified pitfalls in Medicare. Canadians will resolve these with help from India, China and many other countries. All Canadian provinces will increase medical personnel by increasing substantially the number of graduates in the existing Faculties of Medicine, as well as offering free tuition and establishing many more faculties of medicine in other universities.

Canada will address these needs and will save Medicare and Money - there will be NO

MORE of the following:

- Doctor shortage, male or female
- Long waiting lists for surgery
- Hallway medicine
- Difficulty finding a doctor and getting sicker and costing the healthcare system more money
- Flooding of emergency rooms
- Dependency on walk in clinics
- Need for doctor lotteries
- Doctor and nurse burnout or guilty feelings

- Fear of entering the medical profession because of pregnancy and/or family obligations
- Debt because of loans to cover tuition fees and books.

There will be changes and reforms so that the medical profession isn't such a time-consuming profession – drawing the line on overtime hours and more focused on lifestyle. Healthcare teams where physicians, pharmacists, dietitians, and other healthcare professionals work out in one space and share patients will be created. "Collaborative care" – integrating nurses into family doctor's offices freeing the doctor to take on more patients.

Based on Dr Day's study, Canada will fulfill each need by the following:

AT HOME IN CANADA

Federal and Provincial Governments will:

- Retain its doctors and nurses at home
- Open up faculties of medicine increasing greatly the number of graduates
- Establish many more faculties of medicine throughout each province
- Provide free tuition, giving many more Canadians access and opportunity to a chosen profession DEBT FREE
- Implement Chinese and Hindu immersion into its kindergarten programs

VIII.4 - Ban all Nuclear Weapons

Prime Minister Harper will ban all use and creation of nuclear weapons. In doing so, he will secure the support of all Federal parties, namely the Liberals, N.D.P., Green and Bloc Quebecois (Kyoto Agreement). He will now get world attention and lay a foundation for even more allies by using this strategy. This does not hurt Prime Minister Harper's image on the world stage. He will enjoy a world reputation unequalled by any other leader.

Canadians are fortunate and will be very, very proud of their Prime Minister.

VIII.5 - Suspend Tar Sands Operations Ban All Nuclear Weapons

Prime Minister Harper will put a hold on the Tar Sands operation. The amount of water that it requires is both economically and ecologically prohibitive. Because Alberta is a friend of the Prime Minister, they are bound to support his wishes. He will have the admiration and support of all conservationists including Dr. David Suzuki and former U.S. Vice President Al Gore. Canadians will feel confident and secure and know that any problems they have will be resolved by their Prime Minister.

Healthcare teams where physicians, pharmacists, dietitians, and other healthcare professionals work out in one space and share patients will be created. There will be "Collaborative care" - integrating nurses into family doctor's offices freeing the doctor to take on more patients.

Close all oil refineries in Canada and in all foreign countries in exchange for their economic recovery.

Canada will implement laws to restrict/abolish pollution of water, soil and air.

CHAPTER IX:
BROADER HEALTH VISION AND ECONOMIC PROSPERITY

I, the author, will establish Healing Centers designed to focus on all the patient's needs: physical, psychological, spiritual, financial and social. The aim of my program is to live according to His Highness Sri Sri Ravi Shankar's Art of Living Foundation to remove stress.

Physical – The Canadian Government will enforce strict laws on the present food industry. High cholesterol food will be prohibited. Advertising geared to encouraging people to eat prohibitive food will be eliminated. Similarly advertising aimed at young children to eat prohibitive foods will be abolished. We are confronted with a pandemic and/or endemic weight problem which results in; diabetes, stress, fatalism. Relief by eating (adding to the problem) and poor self image. This problem is not confined to Canada but is worldwide. To eliminate this problem the patient can get help by entering the healing clinic at a reasonable cost. A qualified dietician will discuss a diet that the patient will follow while staying at the healing clinic until a healthy weight is reached.

Psychological – It is never a matter of only one thing being the problem but in life it is always an inter-dependency of one thing and another and another and so on and on. This is the prospective that we develop in our lives and what I call "knowing where you are coming from". This helps people to appreciate the fact that the person is who she/he is because of his/her past. We can empathize because we are also a result of our past experience. No one is different in that respect. We are all human beings vulnerable to destiny.

Spiritual – The lesson we must all learn in this realm is that we cannot live without the help from a higher source and to admitting to that fact and to employing meditation. Please refer to pages 8, 38 and 39 of the manuscript for detail.

Financial – The Health Clinic will provide professional help with financial problems. With worldwide economic downfall business is cutting back and employees are losing their jobs. Our professional advices will keep the patient from panicking with an assurance that a program of refinancing will alleviate the problem. Like cutting back on unnecessary expenses ex: Do not buy water, coffee, or meals outside instead prepare these at home.

Social- Health Clinic will provide services for all special occasions, parties for groups as well as for individuals. (Ex: for groups – birthdays, weddings, anniversaries, special days like Bobby Burns, St. Patrick's, Christmas, Easter, Halloween, Cooperation etc. Ex: for individuals- loneliness, depression). Health Clinic will have a Happy Hour (To encourage socializing but will monitor patients diet in conjunction with alcohol consumption and prohibitive foods.

ANCIENT INDA DIET

Ayurveda is a science of restoring balance in an individual n a physical, psychological and spiritual level. The Healing Clinic will test the patients' metabolic characteristics called Doshas (problems). There are three Doshas: Vata, Pitta and Kapha.

Individuals can be classified into one of these or combinations of two or three. Treatment is provided by using Ayurvedic healthcare products. Ayurveda uses herbs, diet, lifestyle, yoga, Vedic astrology, color therapy , energy points – using pressure points, heat and oil, aromatherapy, gemstones, Vastu Shastras (similar to Feng Shui) and various other therapeutic means to promote well being (Sukham)

WEIGHT LOSS

Extremely important in losing weight is listening to your body's needs-What you are craving and what you can't tolerate. If you are craving prohibitive food substitute with lots of fruits, vegetables, carbohydrates like Pasta and rice and/or small amounts of protein (meat or cheese). Having only a small amount of sugar will open up the taste buds and a craving for more. Avoid that by filling up on the substitutes until you feel full. You should never be hungry on a diet.

Now it is where digestion and elimination take place. People are very reluctant to discuss their bowel movements, yet it is singularly the most important secret to losing weight and feeling re-energized. The body is reenergized by the nutrient food. Elimination to maintain a clean bowel safe from formation of polyps which can cause cancer is of utmost importance. The use of Metamucil promotes easy elimination and a clean bowel.

Learning to eat in small portions and often will solve many patients' problems. We must develop a life style of eating to live, not living to eat. I have many very good recipes that are nutritious and tasty. I plan on writing a cookbook. The sales from my cookbook will be reinvested into the Art of Living Healing Centers. People need happier goals for themselves and for their families and their communities. Happier life is needed all around. We need: cooperation instead of competition, peace not war, and contentment not stress. Too much economic stress is too costly.

Solving this problem is enrolling in the Art of Living Foundation and/or start a new Art of Living center in your community.

ECONOMIC PROSPERITY

Canada will open immigration to all countries to promote and/ or enhance big and small business. Employers will receive tax incentives according to the number of employees they hire. Canada will set up systems of local integrations of new comers. To remove stress newcomer employees will implement activities according to their needs.

1. Daycare for their children and/or gardening and cooking for their extended families.

2. Employment for their children.

3. Financial advice.

4. Social activities (Visitors, weddings, parties)

Employees will share a percentage of the profits of their employer. It will be in their own best interest to be efficient and work hard. They will not strike but will work for the common good. To ensure the common good each one must "pull his own weight."

It is not a free ride and each employee must be responsible.

All employers and employees are taxpayers and will add millions of dollars in revenue. The revenue received by the government will not only pay for implementing a program of employment but will benefit from a profit.

NATIONAL HOUSING

Canadian government will implement a strict code of rules for construction of homes. Contractors will be subject to the rules. Government inspectors will be on site to ensure the rules are enforced. Homes will be built of stone and/or of treated lumber.

These materials will last and will be efficient temperature wise. i.e. cool in summer and warm in winter.

To save on green space, homes will be built, in three or four stories high. The first story level will be the employer's home, the second will for the extended family, the third for visitors and/or for storage, the fourth will be for storage of dried garden vegetables and fruits like berries, seeds, mushrooms, garlic, peppers, onions etc. The green space lot will be used to grow vegetables and fruit and to enjoy the outdoors.

GLOBAL WARMING

The Ozone Layer we created has resulted in: skin cancer, added expenses, greater stress, and a lack of a happy life style. Former US vice-president Al Gore with the help of David Suzuki will implement the Kyoto Protocol worldwide before it is too late. (Please refer to page 21 of the manuscript)

CHAPTER X:
DONATING TO THE STEPHEN LEWIS FOUNDATION

I plan to publish my book in English, Hopi, Himdu and Mandarin. This would include the people of China, Canada and India's participation in the plans for change and success.

Stephen Lewis has dedicated his life to serving the public and recently to defending the most vulnerable people of Africa. He has been a politician and a U. N. Ambassador. He has staunchly advocated for the poor and particularly those affected by the HIV AIDS pandemic. Stephan Lewis is truly a dedicated humanitarian who has worked to improve the human condition, both at home and abroad.

There are 13 million children in Sub-Sahara Africa who have been orphaned by AIDS (more than 1/3 the population of Canada). In areas severely affected by AIDS, **approximately ½ of all older people are caring of HIV+ adults or vulnerable children.** 68% of the infections and 76% of the deaths from AIDS occur in Sub-Sahara Africa, the average income is less than $1 per day. In most of the countries of Sub Sahara Africa there is little infrastructure to provide health systems, universal education, support for seniors, even drugs for treatment. You can help!

There are ten-year old female orphans who are menstruating, just when they need their mothers most at such a traumatic time of their lives. They are victims of unspeakable horrendous rape - enough to make one sick at the stomach. They now must raise and feed their younger siblings. Their lives are dependent on our compassion for saving lives. Our lives are "wants" theirs are life saving needs. The money we spend on gifts could be put to better use and in so doing, freeing us of guilt feelings and giving us the satisfaction of knowing we helped to save lives. It doesn't mean we need to give up all gift giving to our families etc, but perhaps we could just make it a little less. It would make a world of difference and you can help.

I have been told that "Rape" is deliberate warfare strategy. Children do not ask to be born. They are our greatest gift. We are given a child that we have done nothing to deserve or earn this child. This is a miraculous event, and to think that there are people in our world who would abuse these innocent children and subject them to this horrific cruelty is beyond comprehension. Hopefully some day, they can be brought to justice!

The Stephan Lewis Foundation needs our help in order to deal with them and the ravages of poverty, civil war and disease. Will you please help – together we can make a huge difference.

The Stephen Lewis Foundation will issue a tax receipt for $10.00 and up, deductions for income tax returns. If you wish to have your gift acknowledged include the address of gift giver.

Elizabeth (Elsie) Hannaford
Castle on the Seine
#501 - 160 Niakwa Road
Winnipeg, Manitoba, R2M 5L1, Canada
Telephone: 1-204-257-2737
Email: hannafor@mts.net

APPENDIX I:
MOVIES, PLAYS AND FAVOURITE TV PROGRAMS

Michael Moore will make a movie titled:
    "Put Your Money Where Your Mouth Is" (Movie)

Alex Gibney
    "Taxi to the Dark Side" (Movie)

Adam Beach
    "Take My Hand" (Movie)

Hal Holbrook
    "Mark Twain" (Play)

Bill Moyers
    "Now" (PBS TV show)
    "Dragon's Den (CBC TV Show)

Charlie Rose
    PBS TV Show

George Stroumboulopoulos
    CBC TV Show

Rick Mercer

Peter Gzowski - deceased
Morningside

BOOKS

Francois Gautier
"The Guru Of Joy"

James Joyce
"Finnigan's Wake"

Marshal McLuhan
"The Gutenberg Galaxy"

Ken Follett
"Pillars Of The Earth"
"World Without End"

Ed Finn
"The Right is Wrong And The Left Is Right"

Erna Paris
"The Sun Climbs Slow"
"Long Shadows"

Jeffery Sachs
"Common Wealth: Economics for a Crowded Planet"

Andrew J Bacevich
"The Limits of Power"

Stuart A Kauffman
"Reinventing the Sacred", Publisher Basic Books

George E Vaillant
"Spiritual Evolution (Random House of Canada)

Susan Neiman
"Moral Clarity" (Harcourt Books)

Jim Stanford
"Economics for Everyone"

Paul Twitchell
"The Tiger's Fang"

Dr Andrew Weaver
"Keeping Our Cool"

John Ralston Saul
"A Fair Country: Telling Truths About Canada"

Thomas E. Ricks
"The Gamble – General Petraeus and The American Military Adventure in Iraq"

Daniel Tammet
"Embracing the Wide Sky"

Jimmy Carter
"We Can Have Peace In The Holy Land"

Dava Sobel
"Galileo's Daughter"

Margaret Macmillan
"Paris 1919- Six Months That Changed The World"

Dolores Cannon
"The Convoluted Universe Book I, II & III"

PREJUDICES AND RACISM

Based on Fear: Seeing only ourselves as chosen race
Multicultural and plural is a Reality within
our species (Human Kind)

Immaturity	World too small for single line vision
Economic Energy	Prosper on cooperation not competition Vision of seeing each other as Humankind with love and understanding, head to heart. Let there be Peace and happiness

MUSIC AND LAUGHTER THERAPY

The Healing Center will have music and laughter healing therapy along with dancing. Music and laughter is not only pleasant to the ear but it penetrates your heart and soul. The most beautiful voices in the world will thrill the patient. Andrea Bocelli, the most beautiful voice of all will thrill you with songs like "Can't Help Falling In Love", "Because We Believe" and "Time To Say Goodbye".

Celine Dion will bring every Canadian to tears with her rendition of "O' Canada". Her unsurpassed superstar voice thrills people worldwide and provides the most wonderful therapy.

Newcomers Ryan / Dan are Canadian identical twins who still possess their boy soprano voices sing the "Theme Song" called "High" of this book. It along with "You Will Never Walk Alone" tells us that together we can succeed.

Rex: Greatest Pianist (Blind)

Russian Folk Songs give meaning and point to the natural beauty of Russia of its rivers and its history.

Three Stooges, "Victor Borge and Carol Burnett are sure to evoke laughter shaking all tension out (so satisfying and relaxing.) And who will get your toes tapping and remind you of our beautiful vast country from one ocean to another but Stompin Tom Connors.

APPENDIX II:
FAMOUS CANADIANS AND OTHERS

Famous Canadians – Past

Art Buchvald
Cora Hind
David Lewis
Dr. Marie & Pierre Currie
Dr. Norman Bethume
Duff Roblin
Flin Flon Miners
Frank Dembinsky
Gabriella Roy
Izzy Asper
J.A. McDonald
Jack Freedman
Joe Brain
Joe Prendiville
Joe Stanfield
June Callwood
Leo Mol
Lew Parres
Louis Riel
Nellie McLung

Peter Gzowski
Pierre Elliot Trudeau
Rod McIsaac Sr.
Sir Fredrick Banting
Stephen Juba
Terry Fox
Thompson Brothers
Tommy Douglas
Whitney Family
William Norrie Q.C

David Collins – Local Trapper

Tom Creighton – Prospector (1914) – Read a part of a fiction novel called Flintabbatey Flonatin.

Famous 5. National Council of Women of Canada

Rod McIsaac Sr. – Donated 1 million dollars to match Steinkoff's contribution to the Centennial Concert Hall in Winnipeg. His picture hangs in the hall in his honor.

Pierre Burton

"The National Dream" CPR Railway Construction

David Northcott, Executive Director of Winnipeg Harvest.

In a presentation to the Senate subcommittee on Cities, May 1, 2008, David Northcott presented Winnipeg Harvest in the following:

"Winnipeg Harvest was founded in 1984 to respond to two conditions: hungry people and surplus food. We believed it was wrong for Canadians to live with hunger in a country with so much. Our goal from the beginning has been to meet the immediate need by feeding people, while working for long-term solutions to reduce the need.

Manitoba food banks provide food to more than 43,000 people every month, almost half of them children. In Winnipeg, the food is delivered to more than 39,000 people through 300 agencies in local neighbourhoods, more than 60 per cent of them based in churches and other faith institutions.

Of those families using Winnipeg Harvest, fewer than half rely on welfare as their source of income. About 15 per cent work, but do not earn enough money to buy the food they need for themselves and their families. Others get income from pensions, disability payments, employment insurance or the alternative economy while many report no income at all.

Many of our clients, despite facing hardships in their own lives, volunteer their time and energy to help others through Winnipeg Harvest. We couldn't do it without the more than 270,000 volunteer hours they give every year.

While redistributing food to people who need it remains the top priority for Winnipeg Harvest, we work to give access to:

- *Free income tax returns for those with incomes under $30,000 (in partnership with a volunteer from the Canada Revenue Agency.)*
- *Redistribution of personal care products and household goods.*
- *Provision of meals and snacks through day cares and other agencies.*
- *New and developing programs to meet the distinct needs of people from First Nations, African and refugee communities.*
- *Training for life and work skills".*

Present Canadians

W. Brett Wilson
Ed. Finn
Neil Young
Helen &Pat Robertson

Adrian Clarkson
David Northcott
Gilbert Robin
Dr. Jon Gerrard
John Ralston Saul
Farley Mowat
Kim Campbell
Justin Trudeau
Margaret Trudeau
David Suzuki
Severn Suzuki
Rev. Bill Blaikie
Celine Dion
Therese Dion
Stephen Dion
Stephen Lewis
Judge Sinclair
Phil Fontaine
Michael J. Hall
Mayor Glen Murray
Susan Ann Thompson
Wayne Gretzsky
Walter Gretzsky
Rick Mercier
Jean Chretien
Gordon Burnell
Howard Pawley
Nick Ternette
Ryan & Dan Kowarsky
Nancy Alan
Frances Russell
William Neville
Gail Asper Paterson
Martin Berge
Miriam Bergen

Lloyd Axworthy
Edward Schreyer
Greg Selinger
Cindy Klassen
George Stroumboulopoulos
Sylvia Ostry
Alma & Ron Gamey
Judy Wasylycia-Leis
Judge Ken Peters
Ray and Audry Pelletier
Rex-Lewis Clack & mother Kathleen

Gerry McIsaac

Successful investor. He managed to convince the TD bank to forgo a million dollar debt that his brother Rod McIsaac Sr. owed. He continues to make good investments and is a very successful entrepreneur.

Bob Brennan

CEO Manitoba Hydro

A few years ago Bob was voted as the most influential person in Manitoba. I think the same holds true today. Bob responds to every concern regarding Manitoba Hydro. He is quick to cooperate with all concerned regarding any problems or concerns. Presently, he is defending Hydro's position regarding world heritage in the western Interlake area & cooperating with the First Nations concerns. Every time Bob writes a letter to the Free Press you can be sure it is very worth reading because he leaves no stone unturned to explain Hydro's position.

Jim Treliving – RCMP Born in Virden, MB

Winnipeg Harvest help never has enough healthy food let alone Candy. Dragons Den, Jim Treliving was working undercover in disguise when he discovered that there were places where they were throwing away donuts because they wouldn't be fresh for the next day and that there are children who are hungry and could use this food instead of being thrown away. Part of the pleasure for the hungry child would be the joy of choosing a donut. It would be like Candy for that child which he couldn't afford.

Errol Black

He is a Professor Emeritus at Brandon University, where he taught for many years in the fields of Economics and Industrial Relations. He is the co-editor of such books as Hard bargains: the Manitoba labor movement confronts the 1990s (1991), A square deal for all: historical essays on labor in Brandon (2000) and Building a better world : an introduction to trade unionism in Canada (2001). He has written several pieces for Canadian Dimension magazine, and has done research for the Canadian Centre for Policy Alternatives. During the early 1980s, Black argued that university president Harold J. Perkins was ruling the university in an autocratic manner, and supported his removal by the Board of Governors. He later served as president of the Manitoba Organization of Faculty Associations in the 1990s.

Al Rogosin

Guided me, giving me confidence and security essential to my success. I viewed him as a "father" figure but he was totally infatuated with me to the point of tears if he couldn't see me. I was so embarrassed but felt sorry for him. He was so very generous with gifts of handmade woolen pullover sweater, crystal vase, fresh flowers and heart shaped chocolate box surrounded by heart shaped garlic sausage and filled with heart shaped perogies. Al had the caretaker let me come up to his room after hours which led to a lot of gossip and stress. He had his room remodeled adding a new rug. His wife innocently remarked it is nice enough to sleep on. I was so embarrassed that he made her apologize to me adding to my embarrassment. We designed a booklet on Native Medicine and laminated the plants and their uses for medical purposes. Al gave me a plant press which he valued so much. I used it to press plants and had a friend in Florida use these pressed plants to make pictures.

I gave one to Al which he treasured. The other 4 which I have and use in my condo décor. I could never have survived at Brandon University if it was not for Al Rogosin. I wish you and yours a very happy retirement. Forever gratefully and lovingly. Yours, Elsie.

Foreign Born Canadians

Carol Burnett
Daniel Tammett
Gov. Gen. Michelle Jean
Hon. Gov Philip Lee
Jimmy Carter
Leo Mol
Michael Moore
Sir Bob Geldof

Home Care Workers

Tara & Dinuk Dias
Elda Borse
Anne & Ray Prior
Anna
Sharon Kulczycki
Ray and Audry Pelletier

Strathclair School Days

Teachers:
Grade 1 Ms. Gladys Sleigh
Grade 2 Ms. Gladys Sleigh

Grade 3 Mrs. Bennet
Grade 4 Mrs. Bennet
Grade 5 & 6 Ms. Pearson
Grade 7 1 year Broadfoot – 1 year Finkbeiner
Grade 9 & 10 – Teacher quit & the substitute was Diamond –
Jewish – Racist towards Natives
High School Principal O.T. Gamey

George Henderson – School Board – Druggist
Walter Zdebiak – Student

Influential Community Citizens

Verna Gamey
Mar Black
Alex Kippen
Dr. Wayne Shoemperlen
Percy Burnell
Dr. Gordon McKenzie

Other Strathclair. MB

Geordie Hogg
Postmaster J.D. Coghlin
The McGregors
The Rapleys
Ross Hogg
Alex Moffett
Watson Twins
Gordon Gamey

Eldin McBain – acted as a minister of Christian service in their
home with family, friends and neighbors.

Bob Wilson – Farmer

Tom Head – Flower Gardener

Ted McBain - Tested my knowledge of meaning of words in the magazine that he brought to our house. I got them correct each time. He was very impressed and brought me more reading material which I used to learn about important things including future vision of Canada..

The Perpeluks – Bill, Walter, Micky, John

Choy Sam – Chinese Restaurant – Bananas – luxury – son moved to Shoal Lake.

Stotharts & Lou Molgats – Clothing Stores.

Credit Union in Strathclair – Dad got advice on investments.

Dick Burnell – Van driver

McCutcheon where my brother Adam worked until he was called to do service. He joined up instead with "Cameron Highlanders".

Margaret Millman - Chuck Duncan

Bing Warrington – Opera Singer

Burt Burnell

He and my father harvested ice for the ice house for summer. My sister Mary was sick and needed a doctor but there was no money, Burt Burnell provided the help needed to save her life by contacting the doctor privately and paying him to treat her thus saving her life.

Mr. Diamond

Taught with a Yard stick in his hand. Hit my brother over the head. He went through the contents of the Principals desk and took his cough drops. I refused to cooperate with him because he was prejudiced towards natives and knew nothing about what it was like to be a native. I complained to O.T. Gamey, our principal and he said I could stay in his room and study. As a result, I was the only one to complete the course and pass the Provincial Exams successfully.

Mrs. Lawrence in Minedosa & son

<u>Neighbors:</u>

Dzivers, Furmans
Harry Dymterko – Strathclair theatre
Leeson – Farmer
Grace Burgess – Student
Muriel Smallet – Student – Died as a result of an abortion
Viola Leeson – Sister Betty?

APPENDIX III:
GLOBALIZATION

GLOBALIZATION

"is a combination of colonization and corporatization, a travesty of democracy!

It is such an affront to the notion of democratic process; it cannot stand the light of day."

*********************=================================********************

There are two ways to rule in our World:

Peacefully or violently (Humanity or war).

It is Time for a Change.

Like Martin Luther King,

"I HAVE A DREAM."